SEYCHELL]

GUIDE 2025

Paradise Found: Turquoise Waters, Coral Reefs

Miguel E. Anderson

Table of content

Introduction

The Seychelles, a collection of 115 islands spread like emerald pearls over the blue seas of the Indian Ocean, has long been on my vacation wish list. It was the ideal place to escape the monotony of daily living, with its clean beaches, rich foliage, and distinct Creole culture. When I finally walked into the powdered dunes of Mahé, the biggest island, I knew this vacation would be memorable.

When I landed at the tiny but efficient Seychelles International Airport, I was welcomed with warm grins and the aroma of frangipani flowers flowing in the wind. My first trip was to Beau Vallon Beach, which is noted for its crystal-clear seas and colorful sunsets. As I walked down the beach, the smooth white sand under my feet felt like silk and the calm waves gave a peaceful backdrop. The sunsets here were unlike anything I'd ever seen, with golden colors smoothly melting into flaming oranges and deep purples, creating a painting that seemed too gorgeous to be true.

The following day, I went on a hike to Morne Seychellois National Park. This enormous park, which covers 20% of Mahé, provided a look into the island's untamed side. My guide, a cheery native called Alain, escorted me through deep tropical woods teeming with rare flora and chattering birds. We progressively ascended to a lookout, where I was rewarded with a stunning panoramic view of Mahé's coastline and neighboring islands. Alain revealed intriguing facts about the flora and animals, including the tale of the Coco de Mer palm tree, whose gigantic, strangely formed nuts are regarded as a national treasure.

A journey to the Seychelles would be completed without visiting the underwater world. I took a snorkeling trip to Sainte Anne Marine National Park, which is just a short boat ride from Mahe. As I stepped into the warm, crystal-clear waters, I was met with a colorful array of aquatic life. Schools of parrotfish zipped across coral reefs, as beautiful sea turtles floated by. The coral gardens were vibrant with hues I'd never believed existed underwater. It seemed like I was swimming in a natural aquarium, and I was amazed by the richness of this little archipelago.

My gastronomic excursion of the Seychelles was similarly memorable. Creole food, a delectable blend of African, French, and Indian flavors, was a delight. I had grilled red snapper with garlic and ginger, octopus stew in a thick coconut milk sauce, and banana fritters coated with golden syrup. The highlight was eating at Marie-Antoinette, one of Mahé's oldest restaurants, where I had a typical Seychellois dinner served in a lovely colonial-style mansion.

My favorite part of the vacation was visiting Praslin, the second-largest island. After a magnificent boat trip, I arrived in the famed Vallée de Mai, a UNESCO World Heritage Site. This old palm grove, often known as the Garden of Eden, is home to the rare Coco de Mer and another unique species, the black parrot. Walking through the dense jungle seemed like going back in time; the towering palms formed a canopy that filtered sunlight, creating dappled patterns on the forest floor.

I took a short boat ride from Praslin to La Digue, an island that seemed like a time-capsule of paradise. The speed of life dropped dramatically here—cars were replaced by bicycles, and everyone seemed to have all the time in the world. I spent the day at Anse Source d'Argent, which is one of the world's most photographed beaches. Its white beaches, flanked by massive granite rocks and caressed by calm blue waves, were just as beautiful in person as they were in photographs. I relaxed beneath the shade of a takamaka tree, sipping freshly cracked coconut water and felt completely pleased.

One of the most unforgettable events of my vacation occurred last evening. I joined a group of natives and tourists for a traditional Moutya dance on the beach. As drumbeats filled the air, dancers gilded hypnotically around a bright campfire. The stars overhead twinkled like diamonds, and the warm sea wind brought the aroma of the ocean. It was a magnificent evening that captured the essence of the Seychelles: happy, bright, and inextricably linked to nature.

As my vacation drew to a conclusion, I realized that the Seychelles had provided me with more than simply stunning images and gifts. It had given me the opportunity to reconnect with nature, enjoy a slower pace of life, and immerse myself in a culture that valued peace and simplicity. The memories I formed there—the stunning scenery, the wonderful welcome, and the feeling of serenity—would live with me forever.

The Seychelles had been more than simply a holiday spot; they had provided a transforming experience. As my jet took off, I looked down at the glittering water below, already thinking of returning to this wonderful archipelago.

Why Choose Seychelles for Your Next Vacation?

Imagine 115 islands spread like emeralds over the Indian Ocean, each one a paradise waiting to be discovered. Welcome to the Seychelles, a location that promises more than simply a holiday; it is an escape into a world where nature reigns supreme and every moment is a picture-perfect memory.

First, let's discuss the beaches. The Seychelles have some of the most beautiful beaches on the globe. Consider powdered white sands that feel like silk underfoot and lakes that are so pristine and blue that they seem almost surreal. Anse Source d'Argent on La Digue is an excellent example, with its famous granite boulders and shallow, warm waters ideal for a relaxing swim. The Seychelles offers it everything, whether you want a quiet place to relax or a bustling beach with water sports.

The weather is another important attraction. With temperatures ranging from 27 to 30 degrees Celsius all year, there's never a bad time to visit. Even during the rainier months, the rain is often short and followed by sunlight, making it simple to schedule your days around the weather.

The Seychelles provide a plethora of activities for individuals who like spending time outside. Hiking lovers will discover pathways that snake through beautiful woods and lead to stunning views. The Morne Seychellois National Park on Mahé is a must-see, with routes ranging from moderate walks to strenuous climbs, all with breathtaking views of the island and the ocean beyond.

The underwater environment of the Seychelles is equally enthralling. Snorkeling and diving here seem like entering an aquarium, with beautiful coral reefs filled with marine life. Sites like the Sainte Anne Marine National Park are ideal for observing colorful fish, marine turtles, and even the rare reef shark.

Cultural encounters in the Seychelles are similarly rewarding. The native Creole culture reflects the islands' mix of African, European, and Asian influences. This combination is particularly visible in the food, which includes octopus curry, grilled fish, and tropical fruits. If you're feeling daring, try the local specialty, fruit bat!

The Seychelles provide a wide range of accommodation alternatives to suit every taste and budget. From opulent resorts with private villas and infinity pools to lovely guesthouses and self-catering flats, there's something for everyone. Many luxury resorts are built on private islands, providing a unique and personal experience.

Traveling around the Seychelles is quite simple. Ferries, light aircraft, and even helicopters make it easier to move between islands. On bigger islands such as Mahé and Praslin, renting a vehicle allows you to explore at your own speed.

One of the Seychelles' distinguishing characteristics is its devotion to conservation. The islands are home to various endangered species, including the Aldabra giant tortoise and the Seychelles black parrot. Visiting natural reserves and protected areas, such as the Vallée de Mai on Praslin, allows you to observe these wonderful species up close and hear about efforts to safeguard their habitats.

A Brief History of Seychelles

Nestled in the middle of the Indian Ocean, the Seychelles archipelago has a history as vivid and varied as its breathtaking scenery. The history of these islands began long before the first European explorers set foot on their beaches. Arab merchants were most likely the first to find the Seychelles, lured by the appeal of the coco de mer, a rare and enigmatic nut that washed up on faraway beaches.

The Portuguese navigator Vasco da Gama made the first known European sighting of the Seychelles in 1503. The first known arrival was conducted by the British East India Company in 1609. Despite this early encounter, the islands were mostly unexplored by Europeans until the mid-18th century.

The French seized legal control of the islands in 1756 and named them after the French Minister of Finance, Jean Moreau de Séchelles. The French era witnessed the arrival of immigrants, slaves, and the production of products like cotton, sugarcane, and spices. The islands' strategic position made them an invaluable asset, and they quickly became a sanctuary for pirates and privateers.

The winds of change blew in 1810, when the British took over the Seychelles during the Napoleonic Wars. The Treaty of Paris of 1814 established British authority, and the islands became crown colonies. The abolition of slavery in 1835 was a watershed moment in the islands' history, causing an economic upheaval. Plantations made way for less labor-intensive crops such as coconuts and vanilla.

The twentieth century saw additional development. In 1903, the Seychelles became a distinct British colony, and the islands started to develop. The development of an airfield in the 1970s paved the way for tourism, which rapidly became a staple of the economy.

The Seychelles achieved independence on June 29, 1976, and joined the Commonwealth of Nations. Political turbulence characterized the early years of independence, including a coup in 1977 that created a one-party socialist regime led by France-Albert René. This time witnessed substantial social and economic improvements, as well as political persecution.

The restoration to multi-party democracy in 1993 signaled a new age of stability and progress. Today, the Seychelles are well-known for their devotion to environmental protection and sustainable tourism. The islands' rich past is mirrored in their colorful culture, which combines African, European, and Asian elements.

Quick facts about the Seychelles.

Welcome to the Seychelles, an archipelago of 115 islands in the Indian Ocean, right off the coast of East Africa. This tropical paradise is known for its beautiful beaches, lush scenery, and rich marine life, making it a popular destination for visitors from all over the world.

The Seychelles is Africa's smallest nation, both in terms of land size and population. Victoria, the capital city on the island of Mahé, is one of the world's smallest capitals, yet it's full of charm and character. You may walk through lively marketplaces, see the renowned clock tower, and explore the stunning botanical gardens.

The islands are a melting pot of cultures, with Seychellois Creole, English, and French being the primary languages spoken. This fusion of cultures is evident in the local food, which is a delectable mixture of tastes from Africa, Europe, and Asia. Be sure to taste grilled fish, octopus curry, and the famed breadfruit chips.

The Seychelles are ideal for nature enthusiasts. The islands are home to two UNESCO World Heritage Sites: the Vallée de Mai on Praslin Island, where the rare coco de mer palm flourishes, and the Aldabra Atoll, the world's second-largest coral atoll and a giant tortoise sanctuary. The Seychelles are a biodiversity hotspot due to its distinctive flora and wildlife, which include the Seychelles black parrot and the Aldabra giant turtle.

The climate of the Seychelles is tropical, with year-round temperatures ranging from 24°C to 30°C. The islands have two primary seasons: the northwest monsoon from November to March, which provides warmer and wetter weather, and the southeast trade winds from May to September, which are colder and drier. This makes the Seychelles a year-round vacation, with the finest weather occurring between the transition months of April and October.

Tourism is the backbone of the Seychellois economy, and the islands provide a variety of accommodations to suit all budgets. There is something for everyone, from luxury resorts on own islands to low-cost guesthouses and eco-lodges. The Seychelles is also devoted to sustainable tourism, with several measures in place to safeguard the natural environment and encourage environmentally friendly behaviors.

Traveling around the Seychelles is quite simple. Ferries, small planes, and helicopters make it easy to travel between islands. On larger islands such as Mahé and Praslin, renting a car allows you to explore at your own pace.

The Seychelles are a safe destination for tourists, with low crime rates and a friendly, welcoming population. However, it is always prudent to exercise normal measures, such as avoiding leaving valuables unattended and being alert of your surroundings.

Plan Your Trip

Choosing the Best Time to Visit Seychelles.

Choosing the greatest time to visit Seychelles is like selecting the ideal moment to enter a dream. Nestled in the midst of the Indian Ocean, this archipelago of 115 islands provides a piece of paradise that entices visitors all year. To properly appreciate its beauty, timing is essential.

The Seychelles has a tropical climate, which means it's pleasant and appealing all year. However, if you want to avoid crowds and make the most of your vacation, try going during the shoulder seasons. April to May and October to November are really enjoyable. During these months, the weather is warm and humid, but rainfall is low, making it excellent for beach activities and island exploration. Furthermore, the islands will be less busy, with lower pricing for lodgings and flights.

The wet season in the Seychelles lasts from December to March. While rain showers may occur often, they are typically brief and give way to bright sky. This season is also hotter and more humid, but the rich surroundings and bright flora make it a lovely time to come. If you don't mind a little rain, you can still enjoy the beaches, snorkeling, and diving without the peak season crowds.

The southeast trade winds, which blow from June to September, help to chill things down. This is the dry season, and while the temperatures are somewhat lower, the weather remains nice. Winds may make the waters rougher, so keep that in mind if you intend to spend a lot of time on the ocean. However, it is also an excellent period for sailing and windsurfing.

No matter when you arrive, the Seychelles provide a plethora of activities and experiences. There is something for everyone, from relaxing on lovely beaches and swimming in crystal-clear seas to trekking through lush forests and seeing enormous tortoises. And, with its distinct mix of African, European, and Asian influences, the local culture is as alive and varied as the islands themselves.

Understanding Entry Requirements and Visas in Seychelles

When planning a vacation to the Seychelles, it is essential to understand the entrance criteria and visa laws to guarantee a hassle-free journey. The Seychelles, a beautiful archipelago in the Indian Ocean, welcomes visitors with open arms, and its visa procedures are intended to make your vacation as simple as possible.

First and foremost, it is worth noting that Seychelles is a visa-free country for all nations. This implies you don't have to apply for a visa before your travel. Instead, upon arrival, you will be issued a visitor's permission, allowing you to remain for up to three months. This permit may be renewed for three more months, giving you a total of six months to explore the islands.

To receive a visitor's pass, you must complete a few fundamental standards. Make sure your passport is valid for the length of your trip and has at least one blank page for entrance stamps. You will also need to provide confirmation of onward or return travel, as well as proof of lodging, such as a hotel reservation or an invitation from a host. Furthermore, you must be able to show that you have enough money to support your stay.

While the procedure is typically basic, there are a few extra factors to consider. If you are going from a country where yellow fever is prevalent, you must provide a valid yellow fever vaccination certificate upon arrival. This is a preventive step to keep both tourists and residents safe from any health hazards.

Those wishing to remain longer or participate in activities other than tourism, such as job or study, may need separate permissions and visas. The Seychelles provides a variety of licenses, including gainful activity permits for work, student permits for education, and resident permits for people seeking to stay permanently. Each of these licenses has its own set of conditions and application procedures, so contact the Seychelles Department of Immigration for the most up-to-date information.

Booking Flights and Accommodation in Seychelles

Planning a trip to the Seychelles is an exciting journey, and booking your flights and lodgings is the first step toward making your ideal holiday come true. The Seychelles, with its beautiful beaches, lush terrain, and lively culture, offers memorable experiences.

When it comes to booking flights, the Seychelles is serviced by a number of international carriers, making it accessible from across the globe. Seychelles International Airport (SEZ), located on Mahé Island, serves as the primary gateway. Direct flights are accessible from major destinations such Paris, Dubai, Johannesburg, and Nairobi, among others. If you're traveling from afar, you may need to connect at one of these hubs. It is recommended that you book your flights well in advance, particularly if you want to come during the high season, which runs from December to March or June to September.

Once you've booked your tickets, it's time to choose where you'll stay. The Seychelles have a diverse choice of lodgings to suit every budget and inclination. From opulent resorts and boutique hotels to lovely guesthouses and self-catering flats, there's something for everyone.

For visitors seeking luxury, the Seychelles has some of the world's most exclusive resorts. Places like the Four Seasons Resort Seychelles, Constance Lemuria, and Six Senses Zil Pasyon provide unrivaled comfort, breathtaking vistas, and first-rate facilities. These resorts often provide private villas, infinity pools, and direct beach access, making them ideal for a romantic break or a special event.

If you're searching for something more affordable, there are several mid-range hotels and guesthouses that provide outstanding value for money. La Digue Island Lodge and Le Repaire Boutique Hotel provide pleasant lodgings with a touch of local character. These places often provide breakfast and are conveniently positioned near major attractions and beaches.

Consider renting a self-catering apartment or villa for a more self-sufficient vacation. This option is ideal for families or groups of friends who desire the freedom to prepare their own meals while enjoying a home-away-from-home environment. Many of these villas are situated in picturesque places, with stunning views and easy access to the beach.

When reserving your lodgings, it is important to consider the location. Mahé, the biggest island, is an excellent starting point for visiting the Seychelles, with its busy city, Victoria, and various beaches and hiking paths. Praslin, the second-largest island, is famous for its beautiful beaches, such as Anse Lazio, and the UNESCO-designated Vallée de Mai Nature Reserve. La Digue, with its laid-back ambiance and prominent granite boulders at Anse Source d'Argent, is ideal for people who want to relax and appreciate nature.

Packing Essentials for Seychelles

Packing for a vacation to the Seychelles entails embracing the island's laid-back atmosphere while being prepared for its tropical environment. This archipelago, with its beautiful beaches and lush scenery, beckons you to unwind and explore, so pack intelligently to make the most of your visit.

Start with the basics: lightweight, breathable clothing is essential. Consider cotton, linen, and other textiles that will help you stay cool in hot, humid conditions. Pack a variety of shorts, t-shirts, sundresses, and swimsuits. You'll be spending a lot of time at the beach, so pack some swimsuits and cover-ups. A wide-brimmed hat and sunglasses are vital for sun protection, as is a high-SPF sunscreen.

Footwear should be both comfortable and useful. Flip-flops or sandals are ideal for the beach, while durable walking shoes will let you explore the islands' paths and natural reserves. If you want to participate in any water sports, carry water shoes to protect your feet from jagged rocks and coral.

Evenings in the Seychelles are often warm, so bring a light sweater or shawl for colder evenings or air-conditioned restaurants. If you're staying at a premium resort, you may want to pack a stylish clothing for dinner, although most restaurants have a casual dress code.

A beach bag or daypack is ideal for transporting your needs on day outings. To remain hydrated, bring a reusable water bottle, particularly if you'll be out in the sun for the whole day. A quick-dry towel is also a wonderful choice for vacations to the beach and on the water.

If you want to explore the aquatic environment, remember to bring your snorkel gear. While many hotels and tour companies supply equipment, having your own assures the best fit and comfort. If you like diving, bring your certification card and logbook.

Pack a simple first aid package that includes band-aids, antiseptic wipes, and any personal prescriptions you may need. Insect repellent is also recommended, since mosquitoes may be a nuisance, particularly in the nights. A small bottle of hand sanitizer is always essential, and if you need to wash clothing during your stay, consider carrying a travel-sized laundry detergent.

Finally, ensure that you have all of your crucial paperwork. Your passport should be valid for the length of your visit, and you should save copies of your travel insurance, airline information, and hotel reservations. If you want to hire a vehicle, carry both your driver's license and an international driving permit.

Budget and Travel Costs in Seychelles

Planning a vacation to the Seychelles is like setting the scene for a tropical adventure, but you must budget carefully to get the most of your trip. The Seychelles, with its magnificent beaches, active marine life, and lush landscapes, might be expensive, but with proper preparation, you can enjoy this paradise without breaking the bank.

First, let us discuss flying. Airfare to the Seychelles varies greatly based on where you travel from and the time of year. A round-trip ticket from major European or Middle Eastern locations often costs between $700 and $1,500. Booking early and being flexible about your vacation dates will help you get a better rate.

Once you've arrived, your next large expenditure will be lodging. The Seychelles has a variety of accommodations, ranging from luxury resorts to inexpensive guesthouses. A mid-range hotel will typically cost between $150 and $500 a night. If you want to indulge, high-end resorts might cost more than $1,000 per night. Budget tourists may stay in guesthouses or self-catering flats for $50 to $150 per night.

Food and dining in the Seychelles might be expensive, but there are methods to save money. Dining at neighborhood eateries and takeout is less expensive than dining at hotel restaurants. Expect to pay $10 to $20 for a lunch at a neighborhood restaurant, whereas a supper at a mid-range restaurant may cost $30 to $50. If you prefer to prepare your own meals, buying at local markets and grocery shops might be a cost-effective solution.

Getting around the islands is another concern. Public buses are the cheapest method to go about Mahé and Praslin, costing just a few dollars each journey. Taxis are more costly, with prices beginning around $10 for short rides. Renting a vehicle is a practical choice for exploring at your own leisure, with daily costs ranging from $50 to $100. Inter-island travel by boat or domestic flights may also add to your budget, with round-trip ferry tickets ranging from $50 to $100.

Activities and excursions allow you to adapt your budget to your specific interests. Snorkeling and hiking are relatively inexpensive, whereas guided tours, diving trips, and boat charters may be more expensive. For example, a half-day snorkeling tour may cost roughly $50, but a full-day diving adventure might cost $150 to $200. National parks and natural reserves often charge low entrance fees of less than $20.

Getting to Know Seychellen

Geography and Climate of the Seychelles

Nestled in the center of the Indian Ocean, Seychelles is a tropical paradise that calls with its spectacular natural beauty and distinct geographical traits. This archipelago, including 115 islands, is a combination of granite and coral formations, each giving its own bit of paradise. The main islands, including Mahé, Praslin, and La Digue, are granitic, characterized by lush, verdant hills and pristine beaches. These islands are the remnants of ancient geological activity, making them some of the oldest oceanic islands on the planet.

Mahé, the largest island, is home to the capital city, Victoria, and about 90% of the country's population. The island's landscape is dominated by Morne Seychellois, the highest peak at 905 meters, offering breathtaking views and a haven for hikers. Praslin, famed for the Vallée de Mai Nature Reserve, is a UNESCO World Heritage site where you may locate the rare coco de mer palm. La Digue, with its easy going ambiance and famed Anse Source d'Argent beach, is a favorite among those seeking peace.

The outer islands, largely coral atolls and reefs, span across a broad region, creating a dramatic contrast to the granitic interior islands. These islands are less inhabited and more isolated, ideal for individuals seeking to escape the hustle and bustle. Aldabra Atoll, another UNESCO World Heritage site, is one of the world's biggest elevated coral atolls and a home for giant tortoises.

Seychelles has a tropical climate with temperatures ranging from 24-32°C. The trade winds impact the islands' two primary seasons. From November to March, the northwest monsoon produces warmer, wetter weather, whereas the southeast monsoon, which lasts from May to September, brings colder, drier weather. This environment makes Seychelles a year-round vacation, while the transition seasons between monsoons, from April to October, are especially delightful, with calm waters and bright sky.

Humidity is a frequent friend in the Seychelles, although the cool sea breezes help keep things agreeable. Rainfall is highest during the northwest monsoon, with January being the wettest month. However, showers are usually brief, giving you plenty of time to enjoy the sun. In contrast, the southeast monsoon brings drier weather and stronger winds, making it ideal for sailing and windsurfing.

Languages and local dialects

Seychelles, located in the center of the Indian Ocean, is both a visual feast and a linguistic symphony. This archipelago, with its rich history and varied people, has a language tapestry as colorful as its scenery. Seychelles' official languages are Seychellois Creole, English, and French, with each playing a unique role in the islands' daily life.

Seychellois Creole, also known as Kreol Seselwa, is the most widely spoken language and the majority of people's mother tongue. This Creole language, derived from French, incorporates African, Malagasy, and Asian influences, reflecting the island's multicultural heritage. It's the language of the home, the market, and the heart, and it's used in daily conversation, local media, and even schools.

English, another official language, serves as the medium of instruction in schools as well as the primary language of government and business. Its widespread use is a result of British colonial rule, and it is still essential for international communication and tourism. Most Seychellois are proficient in English, making it simple to travel and interact with locals.

The third official language, French, has an important place in Seychelles' cultural and historical fabric. Many Seychellois speak French well, and it is widely utilized in formal contexts, literature, and the arts. The food, architecture, and place names of the islands all have a French influence, lending a touch of European refinement to the tropical paradise.

Aside from these three official languages, Seychelles is home to a number of local dialects and languages spoken by immigrant populations. These include languages from India, China, and the Middle East, all of which contribute to the islands' rich linguistic mosaic. This variety is recognized via festivals, cultural events, and daily encounters, where you may hear a mix of languages and dialects reflecting the islands' worldwide links.

Currency and payment methods in Seychelles

When you arrive in the tropical paradise of Seychelles, you will need to get familiar with the local currency, the Seychellois Rupee (SCR). This beautiful money, emblazoned with representations of the islands' distinctive flora and wildlife, will help you navigate the archipelago's financial terrain.

The Seychellois rupee is available in a variety of denominations, including banknotes ranging from 10 to 500 rupees and coins ranging from 1 to 25 cents. The majority of transactions, whether you're purchasing fresh fruit at a market or paying for a cab journey, take place in rupees. Carrying cash is a smart idea, particularly for smaller transactions and in more distant places where card payments may not be accepted.

Credit and debit cards are frequently accepted in Seychelles, notably at hotels, restaurants, and bigger stores. Visa and MasterCard are the most often accepted, but you should always check with your bank about any international transaction fees before traveling. ATMs are provided on the major islands, including Mahé, Praslin, and La Digue, where you may withdraw rupees using your card. However, it is good to have some cash on hand, particularly if you are traveling to the outlying islands.

You have several currency exchange options. You can exchange money at airports, banks, and authorized exchange bureaus. Exchange rates are generally competitive, but it's always a good idea to compare them before making a purchase. While US dollars and euros are widely accepted for exchange, it is best to arrive with euros because they tend to offer better rates.

Seychelles offers a wide range of payment options. While cash is king for minor transactions and gratuities, many companies take foreign money, especially for major purchases such as lodging and excursions. However, paying in rupees is sometimes more cost-effective since it avoids the negative conversion rates that might be imposed to foreign currency transactions.

Tipping is optional, but always appreciated. In restaurants, a service fee is often included in the bill, but leaving a little tip for excellent service is a lovely touch. For other services, such as taxi drivers and hotel staff, a small rupee tip is customary.

Transportation Options: Getting Around Seychelles.

Exploring the picturesque islands of Seychelles is a snap, owing to a choice of transportation alternatives to suit any traveler's demands. Whether you're traveling between islands or exploring the beautiful landscapes of Mahé, Praslin, and La Digue, getting around is part of the journey.

Starting with the main island of Mahé, hiring a vehicle is the most convenient method to explore. The island's winding roads and beautiful paths make driving a delight, and having your own car offers you the opportunity to explore secret beaches and quaint towns at your own speed. Car rentals are readily available at the airport and in Victoria, the capital. Simply remember to drive on the left side of the road!

Taxis are a dependable solution for folks who do not want to drive themselves. Taxis in Seychelles use set rates rather than meters, so it's preferable to agree on a fee before beginning your trip. They are especially useful for airport transfers and going to and from the hotel. While most drivers take credit cards, packing cash is usually a smart idea.

Public buses provide an inexpensive method to get throughout Mahé and Praslin. The Seychelles Public Transport Corporation (SPTC) operates frequent services connecting major cities and tourist destinations. Buses are an excellent opportunity to meet people and learn about daily life on the islands. You will require an SPTC card, which can be purchased and reloaded at bus terminals and numerous retailers.

Island hopping is essential in Seychelles, as boats are the major form of transportation between the main islands. The Cat Cocos ferry service runs daily services between Mahé, Praslin, and La Digue. The voyage is relaxing and provides breathtaking views of the Indian Ocean. Booking in advance is recommended, especially during peak tourist seasons.

Consider flying domestically for a faster transfer. Air Seychelles conducts flights between Mahé and

Praslin, offering a more efficient and picturesque alternative to the ferry. The trip lasts around 15 minutes and provides overhead views of the islands' blue seas and lush foliage.

In La Digue, life moves at a slower pace, as does transportation. Bicycles are the preferred way to get around this small, picturesque island. Bike rentals are available near the ferry terminal and at most hotels. Cycling along the peaceful roads and seaside trails is a great way to discover La Digue's beautiful beaches and attractive communities.

The resorts typically arrange transfers for guests staying on more remote islands, such as Silhouette or Denis Island. These may include private boat transports, light aircraft, or even helicopters, assuring a smooth arrival to your remote paradise.

Essential Travel Apps and Tools for the Seychelles

When planning a trip to a destination as enchanting as the Seychelles, having the right travel apps and tools can make the journey easier and more enjoyable. Here are some essential apps for navigating, planning, and enjoying your tropical adventure.

First and foremost, Skyscanner is an essential tool for booking flights and accommodations. This software searches the web for the greatest bargains on flights, hotels, and auto rentals, allowing you to easily compare costs and discover the best alternatives for your budget. Hopper is another excellent tool for discovering low-cost flights, since it forecasts future travel rates and informs you when to purchase.

Once you've arranged your flights, you'll need a place to stay. Airbnb and Booking.com are excellent resources for discovering a variety of lodgings, from luxurious resorts to quaint guesthouses. Both applications include user evaluations and thorough descriptions to assist you in selecting the ideal venue.

Google Maps is an essential tool for moving about the Seychelles Islands. It gives precise maps and instructions for driving, walking, and utilizing public transportation. If you want to tour the islands by bike or on foot, MAPS.ME is another great option, since it provides offline maps that are especially useful in regions with poor internet connectivity.

TripIt is really useful for arranging your vacation arrangements. Simply submit your booking confirmations to TripIt, and it will generate a thorough itinerary for you, including flight timings, hotel locations, and activity schedules. This software stores all of your trip information in one location, making it simple to remain organized.

Google Translate is an excellent language aid tool. While English, French, and Seychellois Creole are commonly spoken in Seychelles, a translation software can help you comprehend local signage and menus. The app also supports offline translation, which is useful if you are in an area with limited internet access.

Staying connected is essential, and WhatsApp is ideal for staying in touch with friends and family back home. It's also popular among locals, making it an easy way to communicate with your hosts or tour operators.

TripAdvisor is your go-to app for discovering the best restaurants, bars, and attractions. It includes millions of reviews and photos from travelers all over the world, allowing you to discover hidden gems and avoid tourist traps. Yelp is another useful resource for finding local restaurants and cafes.

If you're planning a hike or other outdoor activities, AllTrails is a great tool for locating and navigating paths. It includes thorough maps, user evaluations, and images, so you'll have everything you need for a safe and pleasurable experience.

Finally, Trail Wallet is a useful software for tracking your trip spending. You can create a daily budget, track your spending, and see where your money is going, allowing you to keep in control of your finances while enjoying your vacation.

Exploring Seychelles

Mahé in Seychelles.

Welcome to Mahé, the Seychelles' biggest and most dynamic island. This tropical paradise, with its lush scenery, clean beaches, and rich cultural tapestry, is the ideal location for those looking for both rest and adventure.

Getting There and Around

Your trip to Mahé starts at the Seychelles International Airport, which is only a short drive from Victoria, the main city. Taxis and rental cars are readily available from here, allowing you to explore the island at your leisure. Public buses are also a practical and economical alternative, with routes that cover most of the island.

Exploring Victoria.

Victoria, the world's smallest capital city, is a lovely combination of colonial grandeur and lively Creole culture. Stroll through the bustling Sir Selwyn Selwyn-Clarke Market, which sells fresh produce, spices, and local crafts. Don't miss the famed clock tower, a smaller version of London's Big Ben, or the stunning Botanical Gardens, which are home to enormous tortoises and unusual flora.

Beaches and Nature
Mahé has some of the most beautiful beaches in the world. Anse Intendance, with its immaculate white sand and turquoise seas, is ideal for sunbathing and surfing. For a more private experience, visit Anse Major, which is only accessible by a picturesque stroll via thick forest pathways. The Morne Seychellois National Park dominates the island's interior, where visitors may hike through deep woods and take in panoramic views from the island's highest point.

Island Hopping and Marine Life
A trip to Mahé wouldn't be complete without exploring the surrounding islands. Sainte Anne Marine Park, a short boat ride away, provides excellent snorkeling and diving possibilities. The park is home to bright coral reefs and a wide variety of marine life, including colorful fish, sea turtles, and rays.

Cultural Experiences

Visit the Seychelles Natural History Museum and the National Museum of History to learn more about the local culture. These organizations provide intriguing perspectives on the island's history, flora, and biodiversity. For a flavor of local life, visit a typical Creole festival, where you may enjoy music, dancing, and wonderful food.

Accommodation and Dining

Mahé provides a choice of hotel alternatives, from opulent resorts to lovely guesthouses. Whether you choose a beachfront home or a quaint cottage set in the hills, you'll find the right spot to stay. The island's gastronomic culture is similarly diversified, with restaurants selling everything from fresh seafood to foreign cuisine. Try native cuisine like grilled seafood, octopus stew, and coconut-infused sweets.

Practical Tips

When visiting Mahé, it's necessary to follow local traditions and manners. When not at the beach, dress modestly and always seek permission before photographing people. The native currency is the Seychellois rupee, however all major credit cards are commonly accepted. The official languages are English and French, although the residents also speak Seychellois Creole.

Praslin in the Seychelles.

Welcome to Praslin, the second-largest island in the Seychelles, where natural beauty and solitude rule supreme. This island, frequently referred to as the Garden of Eden, is a refuge for anyone seeking a combination of leisure and adventure.

Getting There and Around

Your visit to Praslin starts with a lovely boat ride from Mahé, the main island. The Cat Cocos boat takes approximately an hour and gives spectacular views of the turquoise ocean and adjacent islands. Alternatively, you may take a short 15-minute flight with Air Seychelles to get a bird's-eye perspective of the archipelago.

Once in Praslin, getting around is simple. The island is small enough to be toured by bus, taxi, or rental vehicle. Buses are a cost-effective mode of transportation that runs frequently between essential sites. Renting a vehicle or bicycle provides additional freedom, enabling you to explore hidden treasures at your own speed.

Exploring the island.

Praslin is home to some of the world's most stunning beaches. Anse Lazio, with its powdery white sand and blue seas, is a must-see. This beach is ideal for swimming, snorkeling, or just soaking up the sun. Another hidden treasure is Anse Georgette, a private sanctuary accessible via the Constance Lemuria Resort or by boat.

Nature lovers will be captivated by the Vallée de Mai, a UNESCO World Heritage Site. This ancient forest is home to the rare coco de mer palm, which has a distinctive double coconut. Wander through the lush trails, listening for the sounds of endemic birds such as the Seychelles black parrot.

Island Hopping and Marine Life

Praslin acts as a gateway to other beautiful islands. A short boat journey will transfer you to La Digue, where ox-carts and bicycles are the principal sources of transportation. You may explore the famed Anse Source d'Argent, which is noted for its spectacular granite rocks and shallow, mild water.

For undersea experiences, visit Curieuse Island, a marine national park. Snorkeling here exposes magnificent coral reefs alive with marine life. The island is also a haven for huge Aldabra tortoises, who wander freely.

Cultural Experiences
Visit the Praslin Museum to get immersed in the local culture. This modest but educational museum explores the island's history, flora, and biodiversity. You may also take part in traditional activities like coconut dehusking and breadfruit cooking.

Dining on Praslin is an experience for the senses. Fresh seafood is a mainstay, and popular meals include grilled fish, octopus curry, and seafood platters. Local eateries and seaside shacks provide Creole food with a view, making each meal an unforgettable experience.

Practical Tips
When visiting Praslin, it is essential to observe local traditions. When not at the beach, dress modestly and always seek permission before photographing people. The native currency is the Seychellois rupee, however all major credit cards are commonly

accepted. The official languages are English and French, although the residents also speak Seychellois Creole.

La Digue, Seychelles.

Welcome to La Digue, a tranquil sliver of paradise in the Seychelles where time seems to pause and nature takes center stage. This charming island, famed for its beautiful beaches and laid-back atmosphere, provides an ideal respite from the rush and bustle of daily life.

Getting There and Around

Reaching La Digue is an experience in itself. Most people come by boat from Praslin, which takes around 15 minutes. The travel from Mahé is little longer, taking around 1 hour and 45 minutes, but the scenery makes it worthwhile. When you get off the boat in La Passe, the island's largest settlement, you'll find yourself in a world where bicycles and ox carts are the predominant forms of transportation. Renting a bike is the perfect way to see La Digue, since it allows you to explore its quaint streets and secret lanes at your own leisure.

Exploring the island.

La Digue has some of the world's most photographed beaches. Anse Source d'Argent, with its distinctive granite rocks and shallow, clear waters, is a must-see. This beach is part of L'Union Estate, which also has a coconut plantation, vanilla farms, and a traditional copra mill. For a more private experience, visit Grand Anse or Petite Anse, where the waves are ideal for bodyboarding and the dunes are beautiful.

Nature enthusiasts will be delighted by the island's verdant interior. The Veuve Nature Reserve is home to the rare Seychelles paradise flycatcher, often known as the "veuve." As you walk through the reserve's pathways, you may see these magnificent birds darting among the trees. Another attraction is the island's highest point, Nid d'Aigle, which provides panoramic views of La Digue and its surrounding seas.

Island Hopping and Marine Life
La Digue's position provides it an excellent base for visiting the surrounding islands. A short boat ride will transport you to Félicité, a private island noted for its luxury resorts and outstanding snorkeling opportunities. The seas around La Digue are filled

with marine life, making it an ideal destination for divers and snorkelers. Explore vivid coral reefs, schools of colorful fish, and the odd marine turtle.

Cultural Experiences

Visit the island's modest yet attractive museums to get a sense of the local culture. The La Digue Museum provides insight into the island's history and traditional way of life. Don't pass up the opportunity to sample some native flavors at one of the island's Creole eateries. Fresh seafood, tropical fruits, and meals flavored with coconut and spices are the order of the day. Try the grilled fish or octopus curry, then wash it down with a glass of freshly squeezed juice.

Practical Tips

When visiting La Digue, remember to respect the local culture and the environment. When not at the beach, dress modestly and always seek permission before photographing people. The native currency is the Seychellois rupee, however all major credit cards are commonly accepted. The official languages are English and French, although the residents also speak Seychellois Creole.

Silhouette Island in Seychelles.

Welcome to Silhouette Island, a hidden jewel in the Seychelles archipelago offering a retreat into nature's embrace. This island, the third biggest in the Seychelles, is a haven for lush woods, gorgeous beaches, and abundant species.

Getting There and Around

Your journey to Silhouette Island starts with a lovely boat trip from Mahé, which takes approximately 30 minutes. Alternatively, a simple 15-minute helicopter trip provides stunning aerial views of the island's rough topography and blue seas. When you arrive at La Passe, the island's major village, you'll realize that walking is the ideal way to explore. Cars are few on the island due to its tiny size and minimal infrastructure, resulting in a calm and untouched atmosphere.

Exploring the island.

Silhouette Island is a nature lover's heaven. The island's interior is dominated by the high peaks of Mont Dauban and Mont Pot à Eau, which are often enveloped in fog. Hiking routes go through deep woods, home to rare flora and animals. The island's volcanic origin lends it a rough appeal, with stunning vistas that stand out against the soft beaches.

One of the island's features is Silhouette National Park, which spans 93% of the area. This protected region provides a shelter for species, including the Seychelles giant tortoise and the endangered Seychelles sheath-tailed bat. The park's routes range in intensity from easy walks to demanding treks that reward you with magnificent vistas.

Beaches & Marine Life

Silhouette Island has some of the most remote and beautiful beaches in the Seychelles. Anse La Passe, near the main settlement, is ideal for swimming and snorkeling. For a more secluded experience, visit Anse Mondon, which is only accessible by a strenuous climb or boat. You may sunbathe on the smooth white beach while exploring the vivid coral reefs right offshore.

The seas surrounding Silhouette are filled with marine life, making it an ideal destination for divers and snorkelers. The island's coral reefs are home to a variety of fish, rays, and even the rare marine turtle.

Dive spots such as Pointe Ramasse Tout provide breathtaking underwater scenery and an abundance of marine species.

Cultural Experiences

Silhouette Island has a rich history that is strongly related to the French colonial period. The Dauban family, who formerly owned the island, left a lasting impact. You may see the Dauban Mausoleum, a stately edifice nestled among the island's beautiful foliage, as well as the renovated plantation home, which now functions as a Creole restaurant.

The island's tiny population is concentrated on La Passe, where you may experience the local way of life. The community is friendly and hospitable, and you'll often find individuals eager to share tales about the island's history and customs.

Accommodation and Dining

Silhouette Island provides a choice of housing alternatives, from opulent resorts to eco-friendly huts. The Hilton Seychelles Labriz Resort & Spa is the island's top resort, with breathtaking beachfront villas and first-rate services. Consider staying at one of the island's guesthouses for a more intimate experience, where you will get individual care and be closer to nature.

Dining on Silhouette Island is a delight for the senses. Fresh seafood is a mainstay, and popular meals include grilled fish, octopus curry, and seafood platters. The island's restaurants often employ locally produced foods, ensuring that each meal is both fresh and savory.

Practical Tips
When visiting Silhouette Island, remember to respect the local ecology and culture. When not at the beach, dress modestly and always seek permission before photographing people. The native currency is the Seychellois rupee, however all major credit cards are commonly accepted. The official languages are English and French, although the residents also speak Seychellois Creole.

Curieuse Island, Seychelles

Welcome to Curieuse Island, a hidden gem in the Seychelles with a distinct combination of natural beauty and historical significance. This little island off the coast of Praslin serves as a wildlife refuge and a nature lover's delight.

Getting There and Around

Your journey to Curieuse starts with a short boat trip from Praslin, which usually departs from Anse Volbert or Côte d'Or. The trek takes around 20 minutes and leads you to the island's gorgeous beaches. Once on Curieuse, the best way to explore is by foot. The island is tiny and easy to navigate, with well-marked paths taking you through its different landscapes.

Exploring the island.

Curieuse is well-known for its enormous Aldabra tortoises. These gentle giants walk freely and may frequently be seen near the ranger station in Baie Laraie. The island is also home to the unique coco de mer palm, known for its unusual double coconut, which may be found in the island's beautiful woodlands.

One of Curieuse's features is the Doctor's House, a magnificently preserved colonial structure that currently functions as a museum. This mansion, originating from the nineteenth century, provides an insight into the island's history as a leper colony. The museum reveals intriguing details about the island's history and the lifestyles of its past residents.

Beaches & Marine Life

Curieuse has some of the most untouched beaches in the Seychelles. Anse St. José, with its fine white sand and beautiful seas, is ideal for swimming and snorkeling. The beach also serves as the starting point for the island's primary hiking path, which leads through mangrove woods and across rocky outcrops to Baie Laraie.

The seas near Curieuse are filled with marine life, making it ideal for snorkelers and divers. The coral reefs are home to a diverse range of fish, and you may even see a sea turtle or two. Pointe Rouge, off the eastern coast, is a renowned diving destination recognized for its diverse marine life.

Cultural Experiences

Curieuse's past as a leper colony lends a distinct cultural dimension to your stay. The remnants of the ancient leprosarium, dispersed over the island, convey a painful narrative of the island's history. The Doctor's House Museum gives a more in-depth insight of this historical period, with displays chronicling the patients' life and medical methods.

Dining at Curieuse is a simple but wonderful experience. There are no eateries on the island, so pack a picnic. Enjoy your dinner on the beach, surrounded by the island's natural splendor. Fresh seafood, tropical fruits, and traditional Creole cuisine are ideal for a seaside picnic.

Practical Tips

When visiting Curieuse, please respect the local ecology. The island is a protected area, with continuous attempts to maintain its distinct ecosystems. Stick to the defined paths, don't disturb the animals, and take all trash with you when you leave. The island's admittance charge helps finance conservation initiatives and is definitely worth it.

Aldabra Atoll, Seychelles.

Welcome to Aldabra Atoll, a secluded and beautiful haven in the Seychelles where nature reigns supreme and human presence is minimal. This UNESCO World Heritage site, situated around 1,150 kilometers southwest of Mahé, is the world's second-largest coral atoll and a haven for a diverse range of animals.

Getting There and Around

Reaching Aldabra is an experience in itself. Because of its isolated position, entry is normally granted via special permissions and scheduled trips. The majority of tourists come by boat from Mahé or other adjacent islands, often as part of a cruise. The trek may be lengthy, but the payoff is an unspoiled natural marvel that few get the opportunity to see.

Once on Aldabra, most exploring is done on foot or by small boat. The atoll is made up of four major islands: Grand Terre, Malabar, Picard, and Polymnie, which are surrounded by a wide lagoon. Walking routes and boat tours are the greatest methods to see the various landscapes and fauna.

Explore the Atoll

Aldabra is well-known for having the world's biggest population of gigantic Aldabra tortoises. These ancient species, numbering around 150,000, wander freely over the islands. Seeing them in their natural environment is the highlight of each visit. The atoll is also an important nesting spot for green and hawksbill turtles, which come ashore to deposit their eggs on the beautiful beaches.

The lagoon, with its crystal-clear waters, provides a sanctuary for aquatic life. Snorkeling and diving here show colorful coral reefs packed with fish, rays, and the odd shark. Tidal canals and mangrove forests form distinct habitats that sustain a diverse range of animals, including the uncommon coconut crab and various bird species.

Wildlife & Conservation

Aldabra is a living laboratory for researchers and environmentalists. The Seychelles Islands Foundation oversees the atoll, which is protected and studied for its distinct ecosystems. The atoll's remoteness has protected its biodiversity, making it an important location for study and conservation.

Birdwatchers will be in heaven here, with species including the Aldabra drongo, white-throated rail, and other seabirds breeding on the islands. Flamingos, herons, and frigatebirds inhabit the atoll's mangroves and coastal regions, forming a complex tapestry of avian life.

Cultural and historical insights

Aldabra is well renowned for its natural marvels, but it also has a rich history. Arab sailors called the atoll, which has been visited by explorers and scientists, including Charles Darwin. The relics of early towns, as well as the tales of individuals who lived and worked here, provide a human dimension to this natural wonderland.

Practical Tips

Visiting Aldabra requires meticulous preparation. Due to its protected status, visitor numbers are highly limited, and permits are necessary. Respect the local environment and follow recommendations to reduce your influence. Bring all of your supplies, since there are no facilities on the atoll. The native currency is the Seychellois rupee, but major credit cards are not accepted, so bring extra cash to cover any costs.

Félicité Island, Seychelles

Félicité Island, located only four kilometers east of La Digue, is a hidden treasure in the Seychelles archipelago. This beautiful granite island, measuring around 2.68 square kilometers, is a retreat for visitors seeking peace and natural beauty. Morne Ramos, the island's highest peak, rises to 213 meters and provides stunning views of the surrounding turquoise ocean and nearby islands.

Félicité's history is as diverse as its terrain. It was used as a place of exile for Sultan Abdullah of Perak in the late nineteenth century after he was deported there by the British. Until the 1970s, the island was predominantly a coconut plantation, managed by a tiny population of around 50 people. Today, the island is mostly abandoned, with the exception of the opulent Six Senses Zil Pasyon resort, which covers around one-third of the island. This resort, with its 30 villas and spa, offers a unique refuge for travelers while fitting effortlessly into the island's natural setting.

The island's name, Félicité, translates to "Bliss," which is an apt descriptor for this tranquil haven.

The island is largely wooded, with lush foliage that supports a variety of fauna. The surrounding seas are filled with marine life, making it an ideal location for snorkeling and diving. The southern edge of adjacent Marianne Island is known as a world-class diving destination, drawing divers from all over the world.

Félicité is one of the "satellite islands" of La Digue, with Ile Cocos, Les Soeurs, and Marianne. Tourists commonly visit these islands, which provide a variety of activities such as beachcombing and visiting marine parks. Ile Cocos, a small islet off the north coast of Félicité, has been a marine park since 1996 and is a popular snorkeling destination.

Félicité is easily accessible by a short boat journey from La Digue. The travel takes around twenty minutes, making it an ideal day trip destination. Once on the island, travelers may explore the beautiful beaches, trek through the thick woods, or just relax and take in the breathtaking environment.

St. Anne Island, Seychelles

St. Anne Island, a treasure in the Seychelles archipelago, is located only 4 kilometers off the shore of the main island, Mahé. This verdant, tropical paradise is the biggest of the six islands that comprise the Ste. Anne Marine National Park is a refuge for nature lovers and adventurers alike.

The French adventurer Lazare Picault found the island in 1742, which marks the beginning of its history. Named for Saint Anne, the island hosted the first French colony in the Seychelles in 1770. It has been used for a variety of purposes throughout history, including a short spell as a whaling station in the early twentieth century, the vestiges of which may still be investigated today.

St. Anne Island is known for its breathtaking natural beauty. The island is covered in lush tropical vegetation, with Mount Sainte Anne reaching a height of 246 meters. This hilltop provides a panoramic view of the surrounding blue ocean and other islands. The island's shoreline is lined with gorgeous beaches, each with its own distinct beauty. Grande Anse, situated on the southwest coast, is a popular sunbathing destination, whilst Anse Royale is noted for its sea turtle breeding locations from November to February.

The island's aquatic life is similarly remarkable. The seas near St. Anne are alive with vivid coral reefs and a wide variety of marine animals, making it an ideal location for snorkeling and diving. The Ste. Anne Marine National Park, founded in 1973, was the first of its type in the Indian Ocean and is now a protected region, assuring the preservation of its rich biodiversity.

Accommodation on St. Anne's Island is associated with luxury. The Beachcomber Sainte Anne Resort & Spa, situated on the southwest point of the island, provides a unique getaway with 87 private villas that are meant to fit harmoniously with the natural surroundings. The resort offers a variety of services, including a spa, a diving center, and various gourmet restaurants, assuring a relaxing and luxurious visit.

St. Anne Island is easily accessible by frequent boat services from Mahé's capital, Victoria. The 10-minute boat journey provides breathtaking views of the neighboring islands and the crystal-clear seas of the Indian Ocean. Visitors to the island may explore its numerous paths, rest on its beaches, and participate in a variety of water activities.

Denis Island in Seychelles.

Denis Island, a quiet sanctuary in the Seychelles, is a 375-acre coral islet situated around 60 kilometers north of Mahé. This private island is ideal for people seeking a balance of luxury and nature. The island is named after the French adventurer Denis de Trobriand, who explored it in 1773. It has a rich history and a dedication to conservation.

The island's scenery consists of verdant woods, coconut palms, and gorgeous beaches. The northern tip is marked by a historic lighthouse, built in 1910 and still serving as a sentinel over the island. The island's interior is a wildlife haven, with giant tortoises roaming freely and a diverse range of bird species, including the rare Seychelles fody and warbler, which were reintroduced as part of conservation efforts.

Denis Island is more than just natural beauty; it provides an exclusive retreat with luxurious accommodations. The island's resort has 25 private beachfront cottages, each designed to provide a harmonious blend of comfort and nature. The cottages are spaced apart to guarantee solitude, and each opens directly onto the beach, providing breathtaking views of the Indian Ocean. The resort prioritizes sustainability, with much of the food served coming directly from the island's farm, including fresh vegetables, fruits, and dairy products.

Denis Island is a water lover's delight. The surrounding coral reefs are rich with marine life, making this an ideal location for snorkeling and diving. The island's waters are also ideal for fishing, with opportunities to catch large game fish such as marlin and tuna. The lagoon on the island is protected and serves as a haven for sea turtles and other marine creatures.

The journey to Denis Island is an experience in itself. The island is accessible by a short flight from Mahé, which provides stunning aerial views of the Seychelles archipelago. When you arrive at the island's grass airstrip, you will be met by resort workers and whisked away to your own house.

Denis Island is a place to unplug from the digital world and reconnect with nature. There are no cellphone signals or in-room internet, enabling visitors to immerse themselves in the island's natural beauty and solitude. Whether you're exploring the island's trails, sunbathing on its beaches, or indulging in the resort's exquisite food, Denis Island provides a unique and memorable experience.

Bird Island in Seychelles

Bird Island, the northernmost treasure of the Seychelles archipelago, is a haven for wildlife lovers and those seeking a tranquil retreat. Located around 100 kilometers from Mahé, this 0.94 square kilometer coral island is a paradise for wildlife and marine species, making it a must-visit for anybody touring the Seychelles.

The island's history is as interesting as its natural beauty. Once called as Île aux Vaches owing to the dugongs (sea cows) that frequented its waters, Bird Island has witnessed significant alterations throughout the years. In the late nineteenth and early twentieth century, it was a guano mining facility, with quantities of bird droppings shipped for fertilizer. Today, it serves as a private nature reserve focused on conservation and sustainable tourism.

Bird Island is noted for its bird population, notably the sooty terns. Each year, about 700,000 pairs of these birds nest on the island, presenting a stunning spectacle from late March until October. Other bird species on the island include fairy terns, common noddies, and the uncommon Seychelles sunbird. The island's dedication to conservation is shown by its attempts to safeguard these birds and their habitats.

The island's scenery consists of lush greenery and lovely beaches. A protected barrier reef surrounds the eastern and southern edges, which are home to a diverse range of colorful tropical species. The remainder of the island is surrounded by wide beaches ideal for swimming and sunbathing. The island's interior is a home for enormous tortoises, including Esmeralda, the world's biggest free-roaming tortoise, weighing more than 300 kg and estimated to be 170 years old.

Bird Island's accommodations are modest but pleasant, with a few self-catering cottages that mix well with the natural environment. These villas provide a unique chance to experience the island as an islander, with the additional benefit of a store and restaurant to meet visitors' requirements. The island's environmentally conscious approach guarantees that your stay is both fun and sustainable.

The journey to Bird Island is an experience in itself. A 30-minute journey from Mahé by light aircraft provides breathtaking aerial views of the Seychelles' blue oceans and coral reefs. When you arrive at the island's little airport, you will be met by the courteous crew and the serene beauty of this remote haven.

Beaches in Seychelles

The Seychelles, an archipelago of 115 islands strewn across the Indian Ocean, is known for its stunning beaches. Each island provides its own piece of heaven, complete with pristine white beaches, crystal-clear seas, and lush tropical scenery. Let's go on a vacation to some of the most beautiful beaches this island country has to offer.

Anse Source d'Argent in La Digue is perhaps the most famous beach in the Seychelles. With its stunning granite rocks, silky white sand, and shallow turquoise seas, it's no surprise that this beach is one of the most photographed in the world. The beach is part of L'Union Estate, a historical monument that includes a classic copra mill and a big tortoise enclosure. The tranquil seas are ideal for snorkeling, and the environment is picturesque.

On Praslin, Anse Lazio is a must-see. This beach is often ranked among the world's greatest, and with good cause. Anse Lazio, nestled amid granite rocks, is known for its clean waters and vast length of fine beach. It's a great place to swim and snorkel, with vivid coral reefs just offshore. The beach is readily accessible by vehicle or bus, making it popular with both visitors and residents.

Mahé, the biggest island, is home to Beau Vallon, a popular beach noted for its boisterous environment. This lengthy stretch of beach is ideal for water activities, including jet skiing, windsurfing, and parasailing. The beach is surrounded with restaurants and bars that serve native Creole food and allow you to socialize with the friendly locals. Beau Vallon is also an excellent location for watching a breathtaking sunset over the Indian Ocean.

For those looking for a more private encounter, Anse Georgette on Praslin is a hidden treasure. This beach is located on the grounds of the Constance Lemuria Resort and needs previous permission to access, but it is well worth the effort. The immaculate white beach and sparkling seas are ideal for a day of leisure. The beach is surrounded by rich flora, which creates a feeling of peace and calm.

Petite Anse on Mahé is another beach that provides a feeling of privacy. This beach, backed by lush woodland and granite cliffs, is part of the opulent Four Seasons Resort complex. The sheltered bay is great for swimming and snorkeling, and the scenery is just spectacular. Access to the beach is largely provided by the resort, but the effort is rewarded with one of the most magnificent locations in the Seychelles.

Anse Cocos on La Digue is a little more off the usual route and requires a climb to access. This quiet beach, with its beautiful waters and smooth sand, provides a calm refuge. The trek itself is an experience, bringing you through lush woods and past stunning beaches such as Grand Anse and Petite Anse. When you arrive, you'll discover a natural pool made of granite boulders, ideal for a relaxing plunge.

Cultural and Historical Sites in Seychelles

The Seychelles, a breathtaking archipelago in the Indian Ocean, has more than simply beautiful beaches and blue oceans. This island country has a rich and varied history and culture, as shown by various monuments and historical places. Let us begin on a tour to discover some of the Seychelles' most important cultural and historical landmarks.

Victoria, the capital, is home to the magnificent Victoria Clock Tower, a miniature duplicate of London's Big Ben. This clock tower, built in 1903 to honor Queen Victoria's death, serves as a reminder of the Seychelles' colonial history. Nearby, the busy Sir Selwyn Selwyn-Clarke Market provides a vivid glimpse into local life, with vendors bursting with fresh fruit, spices, and seafood. It's an excellent spot to take up the ambiance and experience Seychellois culture.

The Mission Lodge Lookout, just a short drive from Victoria, is a tragic historical monument. Originally known as Venn's Town, this was a school for freed slave children in the nineteenth century. Today, it provides stunning views of Mahé's west coast as well as a peaceful setting for reflecting on the island's history. The remnants of the school buildings remain visible, affording a peek into the lives of individuals who formerly lived there.

On the island of La Digue, L'Union Estate is a must-see. This old plantation provides an intriguing peek into traditional island life. You may tour the antique copra mill and kiln, where coconuts were processed for oil, and see the colonial-era plantation home. The estate also includes a gigantic tortoise cage and the lovely Anse Source d'Argent beach, giving it the ideal combination of history and natural beauty.

Praslin Island is home to the Vallée de Mai, a UNESCO World Heritage site. This ancient palm forest is commonly referred to as a "Garden of

islands, notably Mahé, are ideal settings for these occurrences.

Those who want a more organized diving experience will find numerous reputable dive companies in the Seychelles. Big Blue Divers and Blue Sea Divers are two highly suggested choices. They provide a variety of diving tours, from single dives to liveaboard vacations, enabling you to visit various dive sites around the islands.

Hiking trails and nature walks in the Seychelles.

The Seychelles, a tropical paradise in the Indian Ocean, has more than simply its beautiful beaches and blue seas. This archipelago is also a paradise for environment lovers and hikers. The Seychelles, with its lush woods, granite peaks, and beautiful coastline vistas, provides a choice of paths suitable for walkers of all abilities.

Beginning with Mahé, the biggest island, the Morne Seychellois National Park occupies a substantial chunk of the island. The Morne Blanc route is one of the most popular around here. This short but steep climb will take you through deep rainforest to a lookout with panoramic views of the west coast. The trailhead is on Sans Souci Road, and the ascent, although difficult, rewards you with views that extend to the far islands of Therese and Conception.

Another hidden treasure on Mahé is the Anse Major route. This coastal walk begins at Beau Vallon and follows a picturesque trail to the quiet Anse Major beach. The terrain is pretty straightforward, ideal for a leisurely trek. Along the route, you'll walk through lush greenery and granite rocks, accompanied by the sound of waves breaking against the coast.

The Copolia path is ideal for those looking for a shorter but still enjoyable walk. This trail is a moderate climb through the forest that leads to a granite outcrop with spectacular views of Victoria, the capital, and the surrounding islands. The track is well-marked, and the trek lasts approximately an hour each way, making it ideal for a morning or afternoon expedition.

The second-largest island, Praslin, is home to the famed Vallée de Mai, a UNESCO World Heritage Site. This old woodland is home to the unique coco de mer palm and many rare bird species. The pathways here are well-maintained and provide a peaceful trek into the heart of the forest. The main route is a circle that takes approximately an hour to complete, but other side trails lead you deeper into this ancient terrain.

On La Digue, the Veuve Nature Reserve provides a network of paths that traverse through the island's interior. This reserve is devoted to the conservation of the endangered Seychelles paradise flycatcher, known locally as the "Veuve." The paths here are quite straightforward and provide a calm getaway from the island's more popular sections. As you stroll, you will be surrounded by the sounds of birds and the rustle of leaves, providing a fully immersive nature experience.

For a more challenging trek, take the Anse Marron path on La Digue. This track is difficult for the faint of heart since it requires scaling over rocks and wading through shallow water. However, the effort is well worthwhile, as you will be rewarded with one of the Seychelles' most stunning and quiet beaches. The climb takes around three hours each way, so pack lots of water and wear strong shoes.

Curieuse Island, noted for its gigantic tortoises, also provides excellent trekking options. The walk from Baie Laraie to Anse José winds through mangrove woods and along the coast, providing breathtaking vistas and opportunities to witness these gentle giants up close. The trek is pretty straightforward, taking around two hours roundway.

Fishing and Water Sports in Seychelles

The Seychelles, a breathtaking archipelago in the Indian Ocean, is a haven for water sports enthusiasts and fishermen alike. With its warm, clear seas and plentiful marine life, the islands provide a wealth of activities for both adrenaline seekers and those seeking a more relaxing experience.

Fishing in the Seychelles is just wonderful. The seas around these islands are filled with a variety of fish species, making it a popular spot for both deep-sea and fly fishing. Deep-sea fishing excursions are readily accessible, with skilled crews ready to take you to the finest locations. Expect to catch large game fish such as marlin, sailfish, and tuna. The excitement of the pursuit and struggle to land these monsters will linger with you long after you return to shore.

For those who prefer a more peaceful fishing experience, fly fishing in the shallow flats surrounding the outer islands is a must. Alphonse Island is especially known for its fly fishing opportunities. You may wade through crystal-clear waterways while throwing a line for bonefish, permit, and triggerfish. The tranquil setting and the difficulty of capturing these elusive fish make for a gratifying day on the lake.

When it comes to water activities, the Seychelles offer something for everyone. Beau Vallon Beach on Mahé is the primary location for water activities. This popular beach has everything from jet skiing and parasailing to banana boat excursions and windsurfing. The tranquil seas and mild waves make it an excellent choice for novices and families. If you want some thrill, try parasailing. As you are hoisted into the air, you will get a bird's-eye view of the breathtaking coastline and turquoise ocean below.

Scuba diving and snorkeling are excellent options for a more immersive experience. The Seychelles have some of the world's top diving locations, with colorful coral reefs and a plethora of marine life. The Sainte Anne Marine National Park, located off the coast of Mahé, is an excellent location for both snorkeling and diving. You may swim among colorful fish, beautiful rays, and even the rare turtle. The pristine seas and rich marine life make each dive an experience.

Kayaking is another popular sport, providing a tranquil opportunity to explore the coastline and secret bays. Many hotels and resorts rent kayaks for their guests, enabling you to paddle at your own speed and find hidden beaches and mangrove woods. It's a terrific opportunity to go up close to nature and appreciate the quiet of the islands.

For those who like sailing, the Seychelles provides ideal conditions for both beginner and expert sailors. You may hire a sailboat or go on a sailing excursion to see the islands from the ocean. The soft trade winds and quiet seas provide a nice sailing experience, with several possibilities to anchor and swim in beautiful harbors.

No trip to the Seychelles would be complete without experiencing stand-up paddleboarding (SUP). This pastime has grown in popularity in recent years, and it is a great way to appreciate the tranquil, clear seas. Whether you're skimming over a coral reef or paddling along the coastline, SUP provides a unique view of the islands while also providing a wonderful exercise.

Wildlife Watching: Tortoises, Birds, and Marine Life in the Seychelles

The Seychelles Islands, a treasure in the Indian Ocean, are a nature refuge. This archipelago is home to several rare species, including ancient giant tortoises, colorful birds, and diverse marine environments. Let's begin on a voyage across the natural beauty of these islands.

Starting with the famed giant tortoises, these gentle giants represent the Seychelles. The Aldabra Atoll, a UNESCO World Heritage site, has the biggest population of these tortoises. Here, you may see these amazing animals in their native environment, plodding slowly over the countryside. Curieuse Island, closer to the major islands, also provides an opportunity to see these tortoises up close. The island is a national park, and the tortoises wander freely, sometimes approaching people with an interested gaze.

The Seychelles are a birdwatcher's heaven. The islands are home to various unique species, making it a popular destination for bird aficionados. On Praslin, the Vallée de Mai is a must-see. This old palm grove is home to the endangered Seychelles black parrot. Walking through the forest, you may hear their unique sounds echoing through the trees. Cousin Island Special Reserve is another birding hotspot. This little island serves as a refuge for seabirds such as the fairy tern and the white-tailed tropicbird. The island's conservation efforts have also helped the Seychelles warbler, which was formerly endangered, flourish.

On La Digue, the Veuve Nature Reserve is devoted to protecting the Seychelles paradise flycatcher, often known as the "veuve." This magnificent bird, with its long tail feathers and glossy black plumage, is a sight to see. The reserve's pathways provide a tranquil stroll into the woodland, where you may see these birds flying between the trees.

The marine life of the Seychelles is very interesting. The seas around the islands are alive with colorful coral reefs and a variety of marine animals. The Sainte Anne Marine National Park, located close off the coast of Mahé, is an excellent place for snorkeling and diving. You may swim among colorful fish, beautiful rays, and even the rare turtle. The park's protected status guarantees that marine life flourishes, providing a diverse underwater experience.

For those interested in observing bigger marine species, the optimum time to come is between October and December, followed by March and May. During these months, visibility is great, and you may see whale sharks and gigantic manta rays. The inner islands, notably Mahé, are ideal settings for these occurrences.

If you want to see the undersea environment without getting wet, glass-bottom boat cruises are excellent choices. These trips provide a glimpse into the abundant aquatic life, enabling you to see coral reefs and fish from the comfort of the boat. It's an excellent pastime for families and individuals who like to remain dry.

Unique Experiences: Creole Festivals & Events in the Seychelles.

Creole festivals and events bring the Seychelles, a dynamic tapestry of cultures, to life, providing tourists with a unique view into the island nation's heart and soul. The Creole culture, which combines African, European, and Asian traditions, is widely recognized, particularly during the annual Festival Kreol.

The Festival Kreol, which takes place in October, is the centerpiece of the Seychellois cultural calendar. This week-long festival in Victoria, the capital, turns the city into a vibrant hive of music, dancing, and gastronomic delights. The streets are alive with the sounds of traditional Moutya and Sega music, as dancers in colorful costumes move to the rhythmic rhythms of drums and guitar. The event begins with a magnificent procession, in which both residents and foreigners participate, exhibiting the colorful Creole culture.

One of the festival's primary attractions is the Creole Village, which is built up in the middle of Victoria.

You may browse through vendors filled with local products, artwork, and traditional Creole cuisine. The perfume of freshly grilled seafood, spicy curries, and sweet coconut desserts permeates the air, enticing you to try the island's gastronomic offerings. It's a sensory feast, showcasing the Seychelles' diverse culinary traditions.

The Festival Kreol revolves on music and dancing. The Selebo event, hosted in the Stad Popiler parking lot, is a must-see. This music event brings together local bands and musicians to showcase traditional and modern Creole music. The excitement is contagious, with the audience dancing and singing along to the upbeat music. The traditional dances, with their sensual and rhythmic movements, are a highlight, demonstrating the distinctive combination of African and European elements that characterize Seychellois culture.

For a more personal encounter, the Moman Kreativite (Creative Moments) event offers a lovely evening of singing, storytelling, and dramatic acts by schoolchildren. This event, held in Seychelles' International Conference Centre, enables youthful talent to shine while also providing a look into the future of Creole culture.

The Seychelles Heritage Foundation organizes the Batenm Poupet, or "doll's christening," which is another unique event. This beautiful ritual, hosted at the Domaine de Val des Pres, pays homage to a period when acquiring a new doll was a rare and exceptional event. The festival brings together relatives and friends to celebrate with traditional music and dances while also providing a nostalgic glimpse at Seychellois traditions.

Art enthusiasts will enjoy the Zenn Artis Kreolofonn (Young Creolophone Artists) exhibition, which features the works of young Creole-speaking artists. This competition, presented yearly during the festival, celebrates the younger generation's originality and ability, with artworks that depict the colorful Creole culture.

The celebration concludes with the Bal Bobes, a large Creole ball that lasts into the early hours of the morning. This event, held on the festival's last night, is a joyful celebration of Creole music, dancing, and fellowship. It's a perfect conclusion to a week of celebrations, leaving you with lasting recollections of the Seychelles' distinct cultural history.

Savoring Seychelles cuisine.

An Introduction to Creole Cuisine.

Welcome to the dynamic world of Creole food, a gastronomic tapestry fashioned from the rich and various cultures that have coexisted in the Caribbean, Louisiana, and elsewhere. Creole food is a delicious blend of African, French, Spanish, and Native American elements, resulting in a distinct and savory experience that is both familiar and unusual.

Let's start our adventure in the center of Louisiana, where Creole food is most renowned. Imagine yourself in the busy streets of New Orleans, where the air is thick with the tempting odors of gumbo boiling on the stove and beignets frying to golden perfection. Creole cuisine is a celebration of the region's history and people, with each dish telling a tale of cultural fusion and culinary invention.

The "holy trinity" of vegetables, which include onions, bell peppers, and celery, is a staple of Creole cuisine. These components serve as the foundation for many meals, imparting a rich, savory, and fragrant taste. Add to this a copious use of spices such as cayenne pepper, paprika, and thyme, and you have the basis for a robust and characterful food.

Gumbo, perhaps the most famous Creole dish, is a hearty stew that includes chicken, sausage, seafood, and okra. The roux, a mixture of flour and fat cooked until it reaches a deep, rich brown color, is essential to making gumbo. This lends the gumbo its distinctive thickness and flavor. Gumbo, served over rice, is a meal in and of itself, with each mouthful providing a flavor of the bayou.

Another popular meal is jambalaya, a one-pot marvel that combines rice, meat, and veggies in a symphony of flavors. There are two primary forms of jambalaya: Creole, which contains tomatoes, and Cajun, which does not. Both variations are fantastic, with the rice absorbing all of the spices and liquids from the other ingredients, resulting in a meal that is both filling and tasty.

No description of Creole cuisine is complete without discussing étouffée, a dish that exemplifies the region's love of shellfish. Étouffée, a thick, spicy stew eaten over rice, is often prepared with crawfish or shrimp. The word "étouffée" means "smothered" in French, and this meal certainly lives up to its name, with the shellfish smothered in a thick, savory sauce.

Creole cuisine is especially noted for its sweets, which are both luxurious and delectable. Beignets, airy pastries sprinkled with powdered sugar, are a must-try. Then there's bread pudding, which is sometimes served with a creamy whiskey sauce, and pralines, which are sweet treats made with sugar, butter, and nuts.

Creole cuisine is more than simply food; it reflects the history and culture of the people who created it. Each meal exemplifies the Creole people's persistence and innovation, as they transformed the resources and skills at their disposal into something really unique.

Must-Try Dishes & Local Delicacies in Seychelles

Welcome to the gastronomic paradise of Seychelles, where the tastes of the Indian Ocean meet the colorful traditions of Creole cuisine. Nestled in the center of this tropical island, the local cuisine scene is a delicious combination of fresh seafood, exotic fruits, and fragrant spices. Let's start on a culinary trip through some of the must-try meals and local specialties that distinguish Seychellois cuisine.

Begin your gastronomic tour with grilled fish, a Seychelles classic. Freshly obtained from the surrounding turquoise seas, fish such as red snapper and rabbitfish are marinated in a mixture of garlic, ginger, and chili before grilling to perfection. The end product is a juicy, delicious meal that is often served with rice and a tart tamarind chutney.

Another well-known dish is octopus curry, often known locally as kari zourit. This recipe comprises soft octopus braised in a creamy coconut milk curry flavored with turmeric, cinnamon, and cloves. Its creamy texture and fragrant taste make it popular among both residents and tourists.

Ladob is a classic Seychellois comfort meal. This flexible recipe may be both sweet and salty. The sweet variant has ripe plantains or breadfruit cooked in coconut milk and sweetened with nutmeg and vanilla. The savory version, which incorporates salted fish, is also delectable, with a distinct flavor profile reflecting the island's Creole background.

Shark chutney is another interesting local specialty. Despite the name, this meal is more like a salad than a chutney. It is made of boiling and mashed shark flesh blended with bilimbi (a sour fruit), lime, and spices. It is often eaten with rice and lentils and has a distinct acidic and spicy flavor.

Don't miss out on bat curry, a meal that may seem odd but is a delicacy in Seychelles. Fruit bats, also known as flying foxes, are prepared in a curry sauce with spices and coconut milk. The flesh is soft and tastes like chicken, making it a must-try for experimental eaters.

For a lighter alternative, the bouillon breed is popular. This simple yet savory soup is created with leafy greens like moringa or Chinese cabbage and is simmered with onions, garlic, and ginger. It's often served as a side dish or light supper, highlighting the island's fresh ingredients.

Seychelles is also famous for its breadfruit chips, a tasty snack prepared from thinly sliced breadfruit that is fried till crispy. These chips are often seasoned with salt and chile, making them an ideal companion to a cool beverage on a hot day.

To satisfy your sweet tooth, try coconut nougat. This classic delicacy consists of shredded coconut combined with caramelized sugar and may be sweetened with vanilla or cinnamon. The result is a chewy, sweet treat that embodies the essence of the islands.

Finally, finish your meal with a glass of kalou, a local palm wine. This somewhat alcoholic beverage is created from coconut palm sap and tastes slightly sweet and pleasant. It's the ideal way to conclude your gastronomic adventure around Seychelles.

Best Restaurants and Street Food Stalls in the Seychelles

Welcome to Seychelles' gastronomic hub, where the rich tastes of Creole cuisine are celebrated in both elegant restaurants and busy street food vendors. Whether you're eating with a view of the turquoise ocean or getting a fast lunch from a local vendor, Seychelles' gastronomy experience is as varied as its breathtaking scenery.

Let us begin our adventure on Mahé, the biggest island, where you will discover Marie Antoinette, one of Seychelles' oldest and most popular restaurants. This restaurant, located in a lovely colonial mansion, provides authentic Creole cuisine such as grilled seafood, octopus curry, and bat curry. The environment is as pleasant as the cuisine, with a friendly, domestic atmosphere that makes you feel like a member of the family.

For a more modern eating experience, visit La Plage Restaurant in Beau Vallon. This beachside treasure serves a combination of Creole and international cuisine, with dishes like tuna tartare and seafood platters that are both visually appealing and delectable. The open-air location, with tables directly on the beach, makes it an ideal site for a romantic meal or a leisurely lunch.

If you're in the mood for something fast and genuine, Jules Take Away in Cascade is a must-visit. Known for its huge quantities and inexpensive rates, this takeout establishment offers Creole staples like coconut crab stew, smoked fish salad, and BBQ pig. It's popular with residents and visitors alike, and the biodegradable packaging is a great touch for the ecologically aware traveler.

On Praslin, the second-largest island, Coco Rouge stands out. This renowned diner in Baie St Anne has both takeout and dine-in choices. The menu includes a range of Creole delicacies, including the well-known bat curry, and the lively environment makes it an ideal spot to socialize with locals and guests.

The Copper Pot in Beau Vallon is a great place to try Indian food, which is also popular in the Seychelles. This takeout restaurant has a variety of vegetarian and non-vegetarian dishes, the standouts being biryanis and samosas. The tastes are robust and fragrant, making them a welcome change from other Creole recipes.

Street food is an important element of the Seychellois eating experience, and no visit is complete without trying some native delicacies. Victoria Market on Mahé is an excellent location to start. Vendors here offer anything from fresh fruit to grilled seafood and spicy samosas. The market is a sensory explosion, with bright colors and delicious fragrances beckoning you from every angle.

Beau Vallon Beach is also a popular street food destination, particularly during the weekly night market. This vibrant celebration has kiosks selling a range of local delights, including grilled fish and sweet sweets like coconut nougat. It's an excellent spot to sample a variety of dishes while taking in the festive atmosphere and live music.

For a real experience, look for the mobile food trucks that wander the islands. These trucks sell anything from Creole curries to fresh fruit drinks, making it a practical and delightful way to try local food. Keep an eye out for the brightly colored trucks and follow the locals to the best areas.

Vegetarian & Vegan Options in the Seychelles

Welcome to Seychelles, a tropical paradise where the verdant landscapes and turquoise oceans are as appealing as the native cuisine. For those who follow a vegetarian or vegan diet, Seychelles provides a great selection of plant-based alternatives, allowing you to enjoy the island's gastronomic pleasures without compromise.

Begin your tour in Mahé, the biggest island, where the lively city, Victoria, has numerous good vegetarian and vegan options. Bravo Restaurant on Eden Island stands out. This restaurant overlooks the scenic waterfront and serves a range of plant-based meals, including a delicious vegetable curry made with local spices and fresh veggies. The environment is ideal for a relaxing dinner, with breathtaking views of the surrounding mountains and sea.

For a more relaxed eating experience, visit The Copper Pot in Beau Vallon. This popular takeout establishment offers a variety of vegetarian and vegan choices, including rich lentil curries and savory biryanis. The servings are substantial, and the pricing is affordable, making it popular with both residents and visitors.

On Praslin, the second-largest island, the Café des Arts in Anse Volbert is a must-see. This beautiful café serves a range of vegetarian cuisine, such as fresh salads, vegetable stir-fry, and fruit smoothies. The atmosphere is relaxed and creative, with bright décor and a tranquil garden setting that welcomes you to stay and enjoy your meal.

Les Lauriers Eco Hotel & Restaurant in Anse Volbert serves traditional Seychellois cuisine with a vegetarian touch. The restaurant provides a buffet-style eating experience with a diverse menu of vegetarian and vegan options, including grilled veggies, coconut curries, and tropical fruit sweets. The focus on fresh, local ingredients guarantees that each meal is full of flavor.

La Digue, famed for its beautiful beaches and laid-back atmosphere, also boasts some excellent plant-based dining alternatives. Fish Trap Restaurant & Bar in La Passe has a range of vegetarian options, including a tasty vegetable curry and a refreshing mango salad. The seaside setting is ideal for a leisurely lunch, with the sound of the waves contributing to the relaxing mood.

For a fast and excellent snack, visit the street food kiosks in Mahé's Victoria Market. Vendors serve a range of vegetarian delicacies, including samosas, veggie fritters, and fresh fruit drinks. The market is a vibrant hive of activity that provides a real experience of local life and cuisine.

If you're staying in self-catering accommodation, you'll be happy to know that Seychelles has several supermarkets and markets where you can stock up on fresh produce and other necessities. STC Hypermarket on Mahé and ISPC Supermarket on Praslin both have a good selection of fruits, vegetables, and plant-based products, allowing you to easily prepare your meals.

Drinks & Beverages: From Coco Water to Local Brews in the Seychelles

Welcome to Seychelles, a tropical paradise with cocktails as pleasant as the island winds. From the sweet nectar of fresh coconut water to the powerful tastes of local beers, the Seychelles provide a great selection of drinks that embody the character of this lovely island.

Let's begin with the traditional tropical drink, coconut water. Coconuts abound in the Seychelles, and there's nothing quite like drinking the cold, slightly sweet water directly from a newly cracked coconut. It's the ideal way to stay hydrated and refreshed after a day of touring the beaches and beautiful scenery. Coconuts are often sold at roadside booths, as well as marketplaces and seashore shops, where they may quench your thirst.

Takamaka Rum is a must-try for those searching for something a little stronger. This locally created rum, produced in Mahé's La Plaine St. André distillery, exemplifies the island's rich history and culture. The distillery itself is a wonderful destination to visit, with tours that take you through the whole rum-making process, from fermentation to maturing. Takamaka Rum comes in a variety of tastes, including coconut, spiced, and black rum, each with its distinct character. For a real flavor of the Seychelles, serve it neat, on the rocks, or in a tropical cocktail.

Another local favorite is kalou, which is a traditional palm wine created from coconut palm sap. This moderately alcoholic beverage has been a staple of Seychellois culture for decades. The sap is extracted from the flower spikes of the coconut palm and may be consumed fresh and sweet or fermented for a stronger, more acidic taste. Kalou is often served during community meetings and festivities, providing a sense of the island's past.

Beer fans will be delighted to learn about SeyBrew, Seychelles' official beer. SeyBrew, brewed by Seychelles Breweries Limited in Mahé, is a light and refreshing lager ideal for the tropical environment. It is commonly accessible in taverns, restaurants, and stores across the islands. For those who want something different, the brewery also makes Eku, a

German-style beer, and SeyPearl, a line of non-alcoholic drinks.

If you're craving something warm and cozy, consider a cup of vanilla tea. Seychelles is well-known for its high-quality vanilla, and this aromatic tea is a delicious way to enjoy it. The tea is often served with a splash of coconut milk, which adds a creamy richness to the vanilla's sweet, flowery flavors. It's the ideal drink to sip while sitting on your porch and watching the sunset over the ocean.

Coco d'Amour is a one-of-a-kind and delicious delight that should not be missed. This coconut liqueur is derived from the Coco de Mer, a unique and distinctive palm tree endemic to the Seychelles. The liqueur has a thick, creamy texture and a sweet, coconut taste that's ideal for sipping after dinner or adding to a dessert drink.

Understanding Seychelles culture

The combination of African, European, and Asian influences

Seychelles, an archipelago of 115 islands strewn over the Indian Ocean, is a cultural melting pot where African, European, and Asian influences combine to form a distinct and lively civilization. This cultural fusion is seen in many aspects of Seychellois society, from language and food to music and architecture.

The Seychellois people, also known as Seychellois Creole, are mostly of African heritage, with considerable influences from French, British, Indian, and Chinese immigration. The country's three official languages—Seychellois Creole, English, and French—reflect its rich background. The most frequently spoken language is Seychellois Creole, which emerged from French and incorporates African and Malagasy elements. It acts as a connecting thread among the islands' residents.

Victoria, Mahé Island's main city, is a lovely combination of colonial and Creole architecture. The colorful wooden mansions with wide verandas and elaborate fretwork reflect the island's French colonial history, while the British influence may be seen in the governmental structures and school system. The busy markets, where sellers sell everything from fresh seafood to tropical fruits, highlight the islands' rich agricultural tradition and the significance of the water in everyday life.

Seychellois cuisine is a delicious blend of tastes inspired by African, French, Indian, and Chinese culinary traditions. Seafood is a mainstay, and local favorites include grilled fish, octopus curry, and shark chutney. Spices like ginger, garlic, and chili peppers lend a unique bite to the dish, while tropical fruits like mangoes, papayas, and coconuts offer a refreshing contrast. Try the classic Creole cuisine "lab," which is prepared with plantains, sweet potatoes, and coconut milk and may be sweet or salty.

Music and dance are fundamental to Seychellois culture, with traditional forms such as "moutya" and "sega" reflecting the island's African heritage.

Moutya, a dance created by slaves transported to Seychelles, is done to the rhythm of drums and is often accompanied by songs about love, struggle, and daily life. Sega, on the other hand, is a more cheerful dance that blends African rhythms with European tunes, resulting in a bright and addictive sound that will get you moving.

Festivals and festivities are an important aspect of life in Seychelles, with events such as the yearly Creole Festival reflecting the island's cultural variety. This week-long event combines music, dancing, cuisine, and art to create a colorful celebration of Seychellois history. Other significant events include the Seychelles Carnival, which attracts people from all over the globe, and the Festival Kreol, which celebrates Creole culture via a variety of activities and performances.

Traditional Music and Dance in the Seychelles

Seychelles, a tropical paradise with sun-kissed beaches and blue oceans, is also home to a wealth of cultural traditions, particularly in music and dance. The islands' traditional music and dance styles are a colorful combination of African, European, and Asian elements, reflecting the people's eclectic ancestry.

Moutya is one of Seychelles' most renowned traditional dances. This dance has a long history on the island, dating back to the arrival of African slaves. Moutya is done to the rhythm of "tanbotambourya," or goatskin drums played with bare hands. The dance is sensuous and rhythmic, and it is often done at night around a campfire. The lyrics of Moutya songs generally describe themes of love, struggle, and resistance, giving a moving peek into the life of the early Seychellois.

Another famous dance is the Sega, which is more energetic and exuberant than the quiet and somber Moutya. Sega music is distinguished by its quick speed and usage of instruments like accordion, guitar, and traditional drums. The dance has a lot of hip movement and is often done during festivities and festivals. Sega exemplifies the islands' ability to combine African rhythms with European melodies, resulting in a distinctive and captivating sound that is difficult to ignore.

The Kontredans is another traditional dance that demonstrates European influence on Seychellois culture. This dance, which originated in French contredanse, has partners dancing in a line or circle while following a series of scripted moves. Kontredans' music is usually played on violins, guitars, and banjos, and the dance is often performed at formal gatherings and festivities.

In addition to these ancient styles, Seychelles has adopted new musical genres, resulting in unusual fusions like as Seggae and Mouggae. Seggae combines Sega's energetic rhythms with Reggae's laid-back sentiments. Mouggae, on the other hand, is a synthesis of Moutya and Reggae, resulting in a soulful and rhythmic sound that is uniquely Seychellois.

Music and dance are an important part of Seychelles' cultural fabric, contributing significantly to communal life and festivals. Festivals such as the Festival Kreol and the Seychelles Carnival provide excellent opporopportunitiesxplore these ancient art forms. During these festivities, the streets are alive with the sounds of drums and guitars, and dancers in colorful costumes entertain both residents and tourists. These events celebrate Seychellois identity, highlighting the islands' rich cultural past and the resilient spirit of its people.

Art, crafcraftsd souvenirs to take home from Seychelles

Seychelles, with its breathtaking scenery and lively culture, provides a treasure mine of art, crafts, and souvenirs that encapsulate the soul of the islands. As you browse around the lively markets and small stores, you'll discover a wide range of one-of-a-kind products that make ideal souvenirs for your trip.

The Coco de Mer, a huge, double-lobed nut unique to the Seychelles, is one of the islands' most famous souvenirs. This peculiar nut, often known as the "love nut" owing to its suggestive form, is a symbol of Seychelles and makes an excellent souvenir. However, it is critical to check that any Coco de Mer you buy has the required certification since the trade in these nuts is highly controlled to conserve the species.

For those who value great workmanship, Seychelles' native art scene is a must-see. The islands are home to numerous great artists who are inspired by Seychelles' natural beauty and cultural legacy. Stunning paintings, sculptures, and handmade jewelry may be found in galleries and workshops all around the islands. The Michael Adams Studio on Mahé Island is a must-see for anybody interested in the vivid and intricate works of one of Seychelles' most well-known painters.

Handicrafts are another important aspect of Seychellois culture. Traditional goods like wo baskets, hats, and mats made of coconut leaves and pandanus are readily available. These products are both beautiful and functional, showing the locals' ingenuity and innovation. The Sir Selwyn Selwyn-Clarke Market in Victoria is an excellent location to find these handcrafted items, as well as other local products including spices, vanilla pods, and essential oils.

If you want something genuinely unique, try acquiring a piece of Seychellois pottery. Local potters make stunning and utilitarian pieces inspired by the island's landscape and animals. These ceramics make excellent presents and are a delightful way to bring a little of Seychelles into your house.

Local culinary goods are an excellent way to bring a taste of the Seychelles home with you. Packaged spices like cinnamon, nutmeg, and cloves are popular, as are jars of locally created chutneys and jams. Takamaka Rum, made on Mahé Island, is another great keepsake. This locally made rum is available in a range of tastes and is an excellent way to share the essence of Seychelles with friends and family.

The Craft Village on Mahé Island is a must-see for souvenir buying. This cultural center highlights the finest of Seychellois art and craft, with craftsmen showing and selling their work. It's a great location to learn about Seychelles' traditional crafts and buy some one-of-a-kind souvenirs.

Religion and Festivals in the Seychelles

Seychelles, a paradise of gorgeous beaches and verdant scenery, is also a place of great cultural and religious variety. The islands' religious customs and lively festivals provide an intriguing peek into the core of Seychellois society.

The Seychellois people place a high value on religion. The majority of the population professes Roman Catholicism, which is a result of French colonial influence. The island's skyline is lined with stunning cathedrals, the most renowned of which is the Cathedral of the Immaculate Conception in Victoria, Mahe. This enormous edifice, with its dazzling white front and tranquil interior, serves as both a primary place of prayer and a meeting space for the community.

In addition to Catholicism, there are groups of Anglicans, Hindus, Muslims, and Bahá'ís. St. Paul's Anglican Cathedral, located in Victoria, is a notable religious structure that reflects British influence on the islands. The Arul Mihu Navasakthi Vinayagar Temple, Seychelles' lone Hindu temple, is noteworthy for its colorful and elaborate construction, which provides a lively contrast to the primarily Christian religious scene. The Sheikh Mohammed bin Khalifa Mosque serves the Muslim community by offering a tranquil space for prayer and meditation.

Festivals in Seychelles are boisterous affairs that combine religious observances with cultural festivities. The Festival Kreol, which takes place in October, is one of the most major events. This week-long event is a spectacular presentation of Creole culture, including music, dancing, cuisine, and art. Victoria's streets come alive with parades, concerts, and traditional performances, allowing tourists to immerse themselves in the island's rich cultural history.

Another notable festival is the Seychelles Carnival of Victoria, commonly known as the Carnaval International de Victoria. This vibrant celebration, celebrated in April, brings together people from all over the globe to honor cultural variety. The carnival has magnificent floats, vibrant music, and dancers dressed in bright costumes, creating a joyous atmosphere comparable to the famed carnivals of Rio de Janeiro and Notting Hill.

Religious festivals are an important aspect of Seychellois society. Easter and Christmas are joyfully celebrated, with special church services, family gatherings, and celebratory dinners. During Holy Week, Victoria's streets are packed with processions and parades, demonstrating the Seychellois people's great religious commitment. Independence Day, held on June 29th, commemorates Seychelles' independence from British sovereignty in 1976. Flag-raising events, parades, and cultural performances commemorate the day and demonstrate the nation's pride and solidarity.

The La Digue Festival, celebrated in August, is a unique combination of religious and cultural festivals. The festival features the Feast of the Assumption, a major event in the Catholic faith, as well as a variety of cultural events such as traditional music and dance performances, sports contests, and a lively street fair. The island of La

Digue comes alive with events, providing an excellent chance to learn about local culture and customs.

Local Etiquette and Customs in Seychelles.

Seychelles, a magnificent island in the Indian Ocean, is famed not just for its gorgeous beaches and verdant surroundings, but also for its diverse cultural tapestry. Understanding local manners and traditions will improve your experience and allow you to connect more closely with the Seychellois people.

The Seychellois are noted for their warmth and friendliness, often welcoming guests with a cheerful "Bonjour" or "Hello." It is usual to greet individuals with a handshake, and when meeting someone for the first time, a courteous "Enchanté" (pleased to meet you) is welcomed. Respect for seniors is highly engrained in Seychellois culture, thus treating people with appropriate titles such as "Mr." or "Madame."

When visiting someone's house, it is customary to offer a modest present, such as chocolates, flowers, or a keepsake from your own country. This gesture expresses respect and gratitude for the host's hospitality. Seychellois houses are frequently warm and welcoming, and you'll most certainly be given a drink or a food when you arrive.

The dress code in Seychelles is largely informal, however mod, modesty is required while visiting religious sites or attending formal functions. Swimwear is ideal for the beach, but while visiting cities or villages, cover up with a light shirt or dress. Topless sunbathing is not culturally acceptable, therefore avoid it to respect local traditions.

The notion of "Lakwizin," or respect and understanding for others, is important to Seychellois culture. This idea promotes harmony and collaboration among people. Public shows of love are normally discouraged, and you should be aware of your actions in public places.

Seychelles is a hasversified culture, and its festivals and festivities reflect that variety. The Festival Kreol, celebrated every October, is a lively celebration of Creole culture. The week-long festival includes music, dancing, cuisine, and art, presenting a colorful celebration of Seychellois history. During this season, the streets of Victoria are alive with parades, concerts, and traditional performances, providing a unique glimpse into local culture.

Another major festival is the Seychelles Carnival of Victoria, commonly known as the Carnaval International de Victoria. This vibrant celebration, celebrated in April, brings together people from all over the globe to honor cultural variety. The carnival's extravagant floats, vibrant music, and dancers in sparkling costumes create an irresistible celebratory mood.

Religious festivals are an important aspect of Seychellois society. Easter and Christmas are joyfully celebrated, with special church services, family gatherings, and celebratory dinners. During Holy Week, Victoria's streets are packed with processions and parades, demonstrating the Seychellois people's great religious commitment. Independence Day, held on June 29th, commemorates Seychelles' independence from British sovereignty in 1976. Flag-raising events, parades, and cultural performances commemorate the day and demonstrate the nation's pride and solidarity.

The La Digue Festival, celebrated in August, is a unique combination of religious and cultural festivals. The festival features the Feast of the Assumption, a major event in the Catholic faith, as well as a variety of cultural events such as traditional music and dance performances, sports contests, and a lively street fair. The island of La Digue comes alive with events, providing an excellent chance to learn about local culture and customs.

Accommodation Options for Every Budget

Health precautions and vaccinations in the Seychelles

When planning a vacation to the Seychelles, it is essential to consider health measures and immunizations to guarantee a safe and happy experience. Nestled on the Indian Ocean, this tropical paradise is a tourist haven, but it, like any other resort, has its own set of health concerns.

First and foremost, schedule an appointment with your doctor at least a month before your travel date. This provides plenty of time to receive any essential immunizations and prescriptions. Routine immunizations, such as those for measles, mumps, rubella (MMR), diphtheria, tetanus, pertussis (DTP), varicella (chickenpox), polio, and your yearly flu shot, should be current.

Travelers visiting the Seychelles should get Hepatitis A and B immunizations. Hepatitis A may be obtained by contaminated food or drink, but

Hepatitis B is transmitted through contact with infected bodily fluids. Both immunizations are essential for keeping you healthy throughout your stay.

Typhoid fever is another issue, particularly if you want to go off the main route or dine outside of big hotels and restaurants. The typhoid vaccination is recommended to guard against this potentially dangerous infection.

While the danger of contracting rabies is minimal, it is important to think about if you intend to do activities that may involve contact with animals. Rabies vaccine is especially advised for long-term visitors and people who may be exposed to animals.

Yellow fever vaccine is only required if you are traveling from a place where yellow fever is likely to spread. This isn't usually an issue for most visitors to the Seychelles, but it's always a good idea to verify current regulations before you arrive.

Dengue and Chikungunya are mosquito-borne infections found in the Seychelles. If you are staying in a region where these illnesses are common, apply insect repellent, wear long sleeves and trousers, and sleep beneath mosquito nets.

Aside from immunizations, keeping excellent cleanliness and being careful with food and drink use is essential. Drink bottled or boiling water, avoid ice cubes, and consume well-prepared foods. This helps to avoid common travel-related ailments, such as travelers' diarrhea.

Finally, don't forget to include a basic first aid kit with bandages, antiseptic wippainkillerslers, and any personal drugs you may need. Having these products on hand will help you avoid a trip to the pharmacy and protect minor health concerns from ruining your excursion.

Dealing with Weather and Sun Protection in the Seychelles

When you visit the Seychelles, you enter a tropical paradise where the weather is just as important as the beautiful beaches and lush landscapes. Understanding how to deal with the weather and protect yourself from the sun is essential for making the most of your trip.

The Seychelles have a warm, tropical climate year-round, with temperatures ranging from 24°C to 32°C. The islands have two primary seasons: the northwest monsoon from November to March, which provides warmer and wetter weather, and the southeast trade winds from May to September, which are colder and drier. April and October are transitional months with calm seas and clear skies, making them ideal for water activities like snorkeling and diving.

Given the tropical climate, the sun in the Seychelles can be harsh. To avoid sunburn and heat-related illnesses, you must protect yourself from the sun's powerful rays. Begin by using a high-SPF sunscreen liberally and frequently, particularly after swimming or sweating. If you intend to spend a lot of time in the water, consider using waterproof sunscreen. Wearing a wide-brimmed hat, sunglasses, and lightweight, long-sleeved clothing can all help protect you from the sun.

The UV index in the Seychelles is high all year, so avoid direct sun exposure during peak hours, which are typically between 10 a.m. And 4 p.m. If you find yourself outside during these periods, seek shade whenever possible and drink lots of water to keep hydrated. Dehydration may sneak up on you in the heat, so always bring a bottle of water, particularly if you're trekking or visiting the islands.

The weather may be variable, with frequent rain showers, especially during the monsoon season. These rains are generally short and might give a welcome relief from the heat. It's a good idea to have a light rain jacket or poncho to remain dry during these sudden downpours.

When organizing your activities, consider the weather conditions. The southeast trade winds bring colder temperatures and rougher waves, which might impair water-based activities. Conversely, the calmer waters during the transitional months are great for diving and snorkeling, affording superb visibility and plentiful marine life.

Common Scams and How to Avoid Them in Seychelles

When seeing the lovely islands of the Seychelles, it's crucial to be aware of typical scams to ensure your vacation stays as peaceful as the landscape. While the Seychelles is typically a secure location, like any major tourist area, it has its share of opportunistic frauds. Knowing what to watch out for will help you prevent any unwanted shocks.

One of the most popular frauds involves taxi drivers. While most are honest, others may attempt to overcharge visitors, particularly if they perceive you're unfamiliar with local pricing. To prevent this, always agree on a fee before beginning your trip or insist on utilizing the meter. Ask your accommodation for an estimate of the cost to your location.

Another fraud to be aware of is the "friendly local" who offers unsolicited assistance. They may approach you with offers to take you to a certain site or assist you with your bags. While some are helpful, others may want a large tip or direct you to pricey places where they get a fee. Politely refuse such offers unless you are certain of their intentions.

Credit card fraud is another issue. When paying by card, keep an eye on your card and make sure it is swiped in your presence. Avoid utilizing ATMs in remote regions and instead choose ones situated in banks or well-lit, bustling areas. It's also a good idea to let your bank know about your trip intentions so they can keep an eye out for any questionable behavior.

Fake tour operators might also be a concern. These fraudsters may give you a fantastic discount on a trip, only to reveal later that the tour does not exist or is of extremely bad quality. To prevent this, schedule trips with trustworthy providers or your hotel. Reading internet reviews might also help you find reliable operators.

Beach scams are another hazard. Be wary of anyone who offers you your equipment at excessive rates. It's frequently cheaper and safer to borrow equipment from your hotel or a reputable rental company. Also, keep a watch on your valuables while at the beach, since petty theft might happen.

Finally, beware of online fraud. With the increase in internet reservations, some tourists have been victims of fraudulent lodging ads. Always use trusted websites and read reviews from other travelers. If an offer seems too good to be true, it usually is.

Emergency numbers and contacts in Seychelles

When visiting the Seychelles, have a list of emergency numbers and contacts handy. This guarantees that if an unforeseen crisis arises, you may promptly get the assistance you need. The Seychelles, with its stunning beaches and verdant terrain, is a typically safe trip, but being prepared is always advisable.

Dial 999 if you have a medical emergency. This number links you to emergency medical services, which are well-equipped to treat a wide variety of health concerns. The major hospital, Seychelles Hospital, is situated in Victoria, Mahé Island, and provides complete medical services. For less urgent medical requirements, there are various clinics and pharmacies spread over the islands.

In case of fire, dial 999. The Seychelles' fire services are swift and efficient, prepared to react to any fire-related emergency. It's good to know that assistance is just a phone call away, whether you're at a hotel, a guesthouse, or exploring the more distant areas of the islands.

For police help, phone 999 as well. The Seychelles Police Force is in charge of upholding law and order, and they are accessible to help with any security issues or occurrences. They are there to aid you if you have misplaced your passport, need to report a theft, or need any other kind of police assistance.

If you want consular assistance, it is helpful to know the contact information for your country's embassy or consulate. While not every country has a physical presence in the Seychelles, many do have regional embassies or consulates that may help. It's a good idea to verify the contact information before leaving and have it handy.

For general queries or non-emergency circumstances, the Seychelles Tourism Board might be a useful resource. They may give information on everything from local attractions to travel tips. Their headquarters is in Victoria, and they are always ready to help tourists make the most of their stay.

Finally, if you want to engage in any water-based activities, it is advisable to obtain the contact information for the Seychelles Coast Guard. They may be contacted at 429 0700 and are in charge of marine safety. Whether you're sailing, diving, or just spending the day at the beach, knowing how to get there might give you peace of mind.

Respecting local laws and regulations in the Seychelles.

To guarantee a successful and comfortable travel to the Seychelles, it is important to follow local rules and regulations. This stunning archipelago, with its pristine beaches and colorful culture, welcomes visitors with open arms, but it is essential to be aware of local traditions and the legal framework.

One of the first things to recognize is the necessity of environmental stewardship. The Seychelles are known for their natural beauty, and the government takes conservation seriously. Littering is highly outlawed, and anyone found polluting faces steep penalties. Always dispose of rubbish appropriately and participate in recycling initiatives when possible. When visiting nature reserves or marine parks, observe all requirements to conserve fragile ecosystems.

Beachwear is okay on beaches, however, it is regarded unacceptable to wear swimwear in cities, villages, or public locations away from the shore. When you're not on the beach, wear a blouse, dress, or sarong. This tiny act demonstrates respect for the local culture and allows you to fit in more easily.

Public shows of love have to be kept to a minimum. While holding hands is typically appropriate, more personal gestures may be frowned upon, particularly in more conservative settings. It is usually better to err on the side of caution and be discreet.

Visitors should also exercise caution when it comes to alcohol intake. Drinking in public areas, such as streets or parks, is prohibited. Drink at a licensed place, such as a bar, restaurant, or hotel. Furthermore, the legal drinking age in the

Seychelles is 18, so be prepared to provide identification if questioned.

Drug regulations in the Seychelles are quite stringent. Possession, usage, or trafficking of illicit narcotics may result in serious consequences, including long jail terms. To guarantee a trouble-free journey, avoid any drug use.

Always obtain permission before photographing people, particularly in rural regions. Some residents may not enjoy being shot without permission. In addition, avoid photographing important places such as government buildings, military installations, and airports.

Driving in the Seychelles needs a valid driver's license, and it's essential to follow local traffic rules. Drive on the left side of the road and always wear a seatbelt. Speed restrictions are enforced, and driving while under the influence of alcohol is a criminal infraction. If you're renting a vehicle, educate yourself about the local driving rules and restrictions.

Finally, respect the local customs and traditions. The Seychellois people are famed for their kindness and hospitality, and respecting their way of life will improve your overall experience. Participate in local activities, sample traditional food, and courteously interact with the community.

Sustainable Travel in Seychelles

Supporting Eco-Friendly Tourism in the Seychelles

The Seychelles archipelago, located in the center of the Indian Ocean, is a paradise known for its clean beaches, lush tropical forests, and diverse marine life. Beyond its postcard-perfect landscape, Seychelles is a shining example of eco-friendly tourism, with sustainability and conservation built into the very fabric of the sector.

Seychelles' dedication to maintaining its unique biodiversity is the starting point for its eco-friendly tourist efforts. With about half of its landmass designated as protected areas, the islands provide a haven for a diverse range of species, some of which are found nowhere else on Earth. The UNESCO World Heritage-listed Vallée de Mai on Praslin Island is home to the famed Coco de Mer palm and the uncommon black parrot. Visitors may take guided tours of this old woodland, which stress the significance of conservation and the fragile balance of this ecosystem.

Marine conservation is equally important in Seychelles. The crystal-clear seas around the islands are teaming with life, including vivid coral reefs and stunning sea turtles. The Seychelles Marine Conservation Society works relentlessly to preserve these undersea riches. Tourists may engage in eco-friendly activities like snorkeling and diving, where they will learn about the significance of coral reef preservation and the risks presented by climate change and pollution. Many dive operations in Seychelles follow rigorous criteria to reduce their influence on the marine environment, ensuring that future generations may enjoy these underwater beauties.

Seychelles' dedication to sustainability extends to its accommodations. Many resorts and hotels have implemented environmentally friendly methods, such as employing renewable energy sources and instituting waste-reduction initiatives. For example, the Constance Ephelia Resort on Mahé Island has been recognized for its contributions to sustainable tourism, such as the use of solar panels and attempts to safeguard local species. Staying in such environmentally conscious establishments not only provides a luxurious experience but also contributes to the islands' conservation efforts.

Local communities play an important role in encouraging environmentally responsible tourism in Seychelles. The islanders are closely attached to their environment and actively participate in conservation efforts. Visitors are invited to participate in local culture and customs, whether by enjoying Creole food created with locally obtained ingredients or buying handcrafted items from local craftsmen. This not only improves the trip experience but also benefits the local economy and instills a feeling of responsibility in the locals.

Participating in conservation initiatives is one of the most effective methods to encourage sustainable tourism in the Seychelles. Volunteer programs, such as those offered by the Island Conservation Society, allow travelers to help with ongoing conservation initiatives. These hands-on activities, such as planting mangroves, monitoring turtle eggs, and doing beach clean-ups, give a better knowledge of the islands' environmental concerns and attempts to solve them.

Travelers may also make a difference by using environmentally friendly transportation alternatives. Biking and walking are great ways to explore the islands while decreasing your carbon impact. For longer distances, electric automobiles and public transit are available, providing a sustainable alternative to conventional forms of mobility.

Protecting marine life and coral reefs in Seychelles

Seychelles, a gem in the Indian Ocean, is not only a retreat for beachgoers but also a vital sanctuary for marine life and coral reefs. The archipelago's vivid undersea environment is a biodiversity hotspot, making it an ideal location for eco-conscious vacationers. The islands put a high value on protecting this aquatic wonderland, and several projects are underway to ensure its preservation.

Seychelles' coral reefs are among the world's most diversified and thriving. These underwater gardens are home to a variety of marine animals, including colorful fish and stately sea turtles. However, these reefs are in danger from climate change, overfishing, and pollution. The severe coral bleaching episodes of 1998 and 2016, caused by increasing sea temperatures, demonstrated the critical need for conservation initiatives. In response, Seychelles has taken many steps to safeguard and restore its coral reefs.

One of the noteworthy programs is Nature Seychelles' Reef Rescuers initiative. This enormous initiative focuses on coral reef regeneration, especially around Cousin Island. The team has created underwater nurseries to cultivate coral pieces before transplanting them to deteriorated reef sections. This hands-on approach has resulted in the successful cultivation and out-planting of thousands of coral pieces, which assist in renewing reefs and maintaining marine biodiversity.

Maritime protected areas (MPAs) serve an important role in protecting Seychelles' maritime ecosystems. The Cousin Island Special Reserve, for example, protects the surrounding waterways, providing a safe sanctuary for marine species. Regular surveillance and patrolling by professional wardens keep these regions free of illicit fishing and other damaging activities. These measures not only safeguard the reefs but also benefit local fisheries by ensuring healthy fish populations.

Community engagement is another important aspect of marine conservation in Seychelles. Local communities are strongly tied to the water and actively participate in its conservation. Initiatives like the LEAP initiative help locals become stewards of their coastal and marine resources. Locals are urged to become involved in conservation efforts via activities including beach clean-ups, public meetings, and educational programs. This grassroots approach instills a feeling of ownership and responsibility for the environment.

Tourism in Seychelles is also focused on sustainability. Many dive operators and tour firms follow eco-friendly standards, ensuring that their operations do not impact the fragile marine habitat. Tourists are informed about the value of coral reefs and urged to take part in conservation efforts. Snorkeling and diving vacations often include information on how to prevent destroying the reefs and the importance of marine conservation.

Seychelles' dedication to marine conservation goes to policy and strategic planning. The government has created extensive action plans to address the dangers to coral reefs. These initiatives include steps to minimize carbon emissions, restrict fishing methods, and encourage eco-friendly tourism. Seychelles hopes to establish a resilient marine ecosystem capable of overcoming the difficulties presented by climate change by incorporating conservation into national policy.

Minimizing your carbon footprint in Seychelles.

Many people dream of visiting the Seychelles, which has magnificent beaches and verdant surroundings. However, the beauty of this archipelago entails a duty to safeguard its vulnerable ecosystem. Minimizing your carbon impact while touring the Seychelles is not only doable but also beneficial. Here's how you may enjoy your vacation while still being environmentally conscious.

Begin your eco-friendly journey by selecting sustainable lodging. Many hotels and resorts in Seychelles are working to reduce their environmental effect. Look for facilities that employ sustainable energy sources, such as solar electricity, and have water-saving policies in place. Some restaurants even provide environmentally friendly amenities such as biodegradable toiletries and recycling programs. Staying in these green accommodations contributes to their efforts and sets a good tone for your vacation.

Take into account the most environmentally friendly modes of transportation. Seychelles is ideal for touring on foot or by bicycle, particularly on smaller islands such as La Digue. These forms of transportation not only lessen your carbon footprint, ut also let you explore the islands at your leisure, soaking in the sights and sounds firsthand. For longer trips, use public transit or electric automobiles, which are becoming increasingly prevalent in Seychelles.

Dining sustainably is another method to reduce your carbon impact. Enjoy the native Creole food, which often uses fresh, locally produced ingredients. Eating locally reduces the carbon emissions involved with importing food. Many restaurants in the Seychelles are devoted to ecological measures, such as responsible seafood procurement and food waste reduction. Supporting these restaurants contributes to a more sustainable food culture on the islands.

Participating in eco-friendly activities allows you to enjoy Seychelles while also helping to preserve its natural beauty. Snorkeling and diving are popular sports, but it is critical to choose operators that use sustainable techniques. Look for those who educate their visitors on coral reef conservation and implement standards to avoid reef damage. You may also participate in conservation efforts that directly benefit the environment, such as beach clean-ups or tree-planting campaigns.

One significant endeavor is the Green Footprint Seychelles program, which enables tourists to offset the carbon footprint of their flights by planting trees. The Seychelles Parks and Gardens Authority is running this initiative, which entails planting native and endemic trees in specified places such as Morne Seychellois National Park. Participating not only helps to sequester carbon but also supports the restoration of local ecosystems.

Reducing waste is another critical component of lowering your carbon footprint. Carry a reusable water bottle and refill it at the hotel or approved stations. This minimizes the need for single-use plastic bottles, which are a major cause of pollution. Similarly, carry reusable shopping bags and avoid goods with unnecessary packing. Many stores and marketplaces in Seychelles are adopting more sustainable methods, and your purchases may contribute to this beneficial trend.

Finally, be cautious of your energy use. Simple acts, such as turning off lights and air conditioning when you leave your room, may make a significant impact. Many hotels have energy-saving measures in place, such as key card systems for controlling power use. Being careful of your energy use helps to lessen the total carbon impact of your stay.

Responsible Wildlife Encounters in Seychelles.

Seychelles, a gorgeous archipelago in the Indian Ocean, is a nature lover's heaven. Its distinct biodiversity and clean settings make it a perfect location for individuals looking for ethical animal encounters. From enormous tortoises to rare birds, Seychelles provides countless possibilities to see its wonderful wildlife while assuring its preservation and conservation.

Seeing the enormous Aldabra tortoises is one of Seychelles' most renowned wildlife encounters. These gentle giants may be found on various islands, and Curieuse Island is one of the greatest sites to watch them up close. You can walk among these ancient creatures, some of which are over 100 years old. The island is a national park, so the tortoises may travel freely in their natural environment. Guided tours give information about the conservation initiatives that have helped save these wonderful species from extinction.

Birdwatchers will discover Seychelles to be an absolute heaven. The islands are home to numerous unique bird species, including the Seychelles magpie-robin and Seychelles warbler. Cousin Island Special Reserve is a must-see for bird watchers. Nature Seychelles manages this protected area, which serves as a haven for a variety of rare and endangered species. Guided tours provide an opportunity to observe these birds in their native habitat while learning about the current conservation programs that work to protect their numbers.

The marine life in Seychelles is similarly intriguing. The crystal-clear seas are alive with colorful coral reefs and a wide variety of marine animals. Snorkeling and diving are popular activities, but it is critical to select operators who use environmentally friendly practices. Many dive centers in Seychelles promote sustainable tourism and teach visitors how to interact responsibly with marine life. For example, they highlight the need to avoid touching or harming coral reefs and keep a safe distance from aquatic wildlife.

One of the most enjoyable nature experiences in Seychelles is seeing sea turtles nest and hatch. Several beaches, including those on North Island and Bird Island, are major breeding areas for hawksbill and green turtles. During the nesting season, which normally lasts from October to February, organized trips enable tourists to see these majestic animals as they come ashore to lay eggs. Conservation organizations work tirelessly to protect these nesting sites and ensure that hatchlings survive.

Seychelles also provides an opportunity to participate in hands-on conservation efforts. Volunteering with local organizations like the Island Conservation Society allows visitors to directly contribute to wildlife conservation efforts. Turtle nest monitoring, bird surveys, and habitat restoration projects are some of the possible activities. These encounters give a more in-depth knowledge of the issues that Seychelles' wildlife faces, as well as the attempts to overcome them.

When visiting the Seychelles, you must respect the wildlife and their habitats. Simple acts, such as avoiding feeding animals, maintaining a safe distance, and following the advice of local experts, may have a huge impact. Visitors who support responsible tourism practices help to guarantee that the Seychelles remain a haven for its unique and diversified wildlife.

Local Conservation Projects You Can Join in Seychelles

Seychelles, with its stunning beaches and verdant scenery, is not simply a sanctuary for visitors but also a center for conservation enthusiasts. The islands are home to several programs committed to maintaining their distinct ecosystems, and visitors can become involved in significant ways. Here's a look at some of the local conservation initiatives you may get involved in in Seychelles.

One of the noteworthy efforts is the Nature Seychelles' Reef Rescuers Initiative. This initiative focuses on coral reef rehabilitation, notably around Cousin Island. Volunteers may engage in initiatives like coral gardening, which involves growing coral fragments in underwater nurseries before transplanting them to damaged reef regions. This hands-on approach not only helps to rebuild the reefs but also gives participants a better knowledge of marine conservation initiatives.

For people interested in terrestrial conservation, the Island Conservation Society provides different volunteer options. On Aride Island, volunteers may participate in activities including monitoring seabird populations, doing habitat restoration, and aiding with the conservation of endangered species. This project is great for bird aficionados since Aride is home to one of the most significant seabird colonies in the Indian Ocean.

Marine conservation is a prominent priority in Seychelles, and the Marine Conservation Society Seychelles (MCSS) undertakes various initiatives that accept volunteer participation. One important effort is the sea turtle monitoring program. Volunteers may assist monitor nesting turtles, protect nests from predators, and gather information on turtle behavior. This effort is critical to the protection of hawksbill and green turtles, both of which are endangered species.

Another intriguing potential is the Seychelles Conservation and Climate Adaptation Trust's (SeyCCAT) programs. SeyCCAT sponsors a variety of activities to safeguard marine and coastal environments. Volunteers may participate in initiatives like mangrove restoration, which protects coasts from erosion and offers critical habitat for marine life. These initiatives often include planting mangrove seedlings and monitoring their progress, providing a hands-on opportunity to contribute to environmental protection.

For people interested in marine life, Global Vision International (GVI) operates a marine conservation program at Cap Ternay. Volunteers may take part in underwater surveys that gather information on fish numbers, coral health, and other marine animals. This information is critical for guiding conservation efforts and sustaining the long-term health of Seychelles' marine ecosystems. The program also includes educational components, where volunteers learn about marine biology and conservation strategies.

The Seychelles also provide chances for people interested in community-based conservation. The Local Empowerment for Accelerated Development (LEAD) initiative aims to engage local people in conservation efforts. Volunteers may collaborate with locals on projects including beach cleanups, environmental education programs, and sustainable agricultural efforts. This method not only helps to safeguard the environment but also promotes local livelihoods and builds a feeling of communal responsibility.

Accommodations for All Budgets

Luxury resorts and villas in the Seychelles

Nestled in the heart of the Indian Ocean, the Seychelles archipelago is a haven of pristine beaches, lush landscapes, and luxurious retreats. If you're looking for a retreat where extravagance meets natural beauty, the luxury resorts and villas in Seychelles provide an unforgettable experience.

The Anantara Maia Seychelles Villas, located on Mahé Island, is first on the list. This resort is a haven of peace, located on the quiet Anse Louis beach. The turquoise waves and silky white dunes make an ideal setting for leisure. Each villa is meant to fit in with its natural surroundings, providing solitude and beautiful views. The professional butler service anticipates all of your needs, enabling you to relax. Whether you're relaxing by your pool or enjoying a spa treatment, the experience is personalized to your preferences.

Next up is Constance Ephelia, who also lives in Mahé. This resort is set over two of the island's most magnificent beaches, both of which overlook the Port LauMarine National Parkpark. The accommodations vary from tropical garden view rooms to magnificent hillside villas, each with a distinct view of the lush environment and beautiful lagoons. The resort's spa town is a refuge for relaxation, while the many dining choices provide a gourmet trip through local and foreign tastes. For families, the Constance Kids Club provides a variety of activities to ensure that everyone has a pleasant visit.

The Kempinski Seychelles Resort, nestled on the famed Baie Lazare, is another hidden treasure. This resort mixes Creole friendliness with contemporary luxury, situated against the background of a quiet bay and a stunning mountain range. The resort is great for both romantic getaways and family holidays, providing a range of activities from water sports to nature walks. The large rooms and suites are built for comfort and provide breathtaking views of the ocean or the beautiful grounds. The resort's restaurants feature a mix of local and foreign cuisine, guaranteeing a great dining experience.

For those seeking an intimate retreat, JA Enchanted Island Resort is a fantastic alternative. Situated in the center of the Ste. Anne Marine National Park, this resort provides a secluded island experience. The villas are fashioned in a typical Creole architecture, with private pools and direct beach access. The resort's restaurant delivers a variety of Creole and international meals made using fresh local ingredients. Kayaking, snorkeling, and visiting the marine park are among the activities available, making it an excellent choice for both leisure and adventure.

Mid-Range Hotels and Guesthouses in Seychelles

Seychelles, with its gorgeous archipelago of 115 islands, has a wide selection of lodgings to suit all budgets and interests. For guests looking for comfort without breaking the bank, Seychelles' mid-range hotels and guesthouses strike an ideal blend between cost and quality.

One notable choice is the Avani Barbarons Seychelles Resort on Mahé Island. This resort is located on the scenic Barbarons Beach and provides a tranquil vacation with contemporary conveniences. The apartments are large and attractively constructed, with individual balconies overlooking the verdant gardens or the turquoise ocean. The resort has a huge outdoor pool, a well-equipped fitness center, and a spa with a range of treatments. Dining at Avani is a delight, with various restaurants providing a variety of local and foreign dishes.

Another excellent option is the Coral Strand Smart Choice Hotel, which is situated on the popular Beau Vallon Beach. This hotel is ideal for people looking to be near the action since Beau Vallon is renowned for its lively environment and water sports activities. The rooms are pleasant and equipped with all required conveniences, such as minibars and private balconies. The hotel's beachfront restaurant is a highlight, serving wonderful meals with views of the ocean. In addition, the Coral Strand has live music and cultural acts, giving tourists a taste of local entertainment.

For a more personal experience, try staying at Blue Hill, a beautiful guest house tucked in the Victoria Hills. This boutique property provides a tranquil escape with breathtaking views of the surrounding area. The rooms are attractively designed, combining contemporary amenities with traditional Seychellois elements. Guests may have a substantial breakfast on the patio while admiring the spectacular views of the island. Blue Hill is also conveniently positioned near the Seychelles National Botanical Gardens, providing it an excellent starting point for exploring Mahé's natural beauties.

The Palm Beach Hotel on Praslin provides a nice mid-range choice. This hotel, located on the lovely Grand Anse Beach, offers a relaxing ambiance while yet providing convenient access to the island's attractions. The rooms are light and airy, with balconies that provide breathtaking views of the beach or the beautiful gardens. The hotel's restaurant delivers a wide range of meals, with a focus on fresh seafood and Creole cuisine. Guests may also benefit from the hotel's outdoor pool and water sports facilities.

For those visiting La Digue, the Chateau St Cloud is an excellent option. This beautiful hotel is housed in a historic plantation home and surrounded by gorgeous tropical gardens. The rooms are generously sized and attractively appointed, providing a pleasant stay with a touch of colonial elegance. The hotel's restaurant serves delectable Creole cuisine, and the outdoor pool offers a welcome respite from the tropical heat. Chateau St Cloud is a great location for exploring the island, with La Digue's famed Anse Source d'Argent beach just a short bike ride away.

Budget-Friendly Accommodation & Hostels

Seychelles, a tropical paradise in the Indian Ocean, is typically associated with luxury, but it also has a variety of affordable hotels that enable visitors to enjoy its beauty without breaking the bank. There are several alternatives for people wishing to visit this beautiful archipelago on a budget, ranging from charming guest houses to economical hotels.

Bel Air Hotel in Victoria, Mahé, is one of the greatest value-for-money alternatives. This quaint hotel has pleasant rooms with air conditioning, minibars, and kitchenettes. The hotel is strategically positioned near renowned sites such as the Seychelles National Botanical Gardens and Victoria Market, giving it an excellent starting point for touring the island. Guests may enjoy free Wi-Fi and parking, and the on-site restaurant delivers wonderful meals, offering a comfortable stay at a reasonable price.

Takamaka Green Village, located in the south of Mahé, offers a more rural experience. This hotel is situated in a serene setting, surrounded by beautiful gardens and orchards. The rooms are basic yet cozy, with furniture made by local artists. Guests may have a delicious breakfast in the garden before visiting neighboring sites such as Anse Takamaka Beach and hiking routes to Anse Capuccins or Police Bay. The courteous hosts create a warm and inviting environment, making it an ideal destination for budget-conscious tourists.

Captain's Villa is another wonderful alternative, situated on Mahé's southeast coast near Anse Forbans beach. This family-run guesthouse has large apartments with fully equipped kitchens, air-conditioned bedrooms, and relaxing lounge spaces. The neighboring food shops and restaurants make it simple to cook your meals or go out. The beach is just a short walk away, offering plenty of options for snorkeling and enjoying the turquoise seas.

On Praslin Island, Villa Anse La Blague provides low-cost accommodation with breathtaking ocean views. This guesthouse has nice rooms with its balconies where you can relax and enjoy the peaceful surroundings. The on-site restaurant provides a variety of local foods, and the helpful staff can help you plan activities such as snorkeling, diving, and island excursions. The peaceful setting makes it a great hideaway for anyone wishing to rest and unwind without breaking the bank.

Pension Fidele is a great value for guests visiting La Digue. This guesthouse is set in a tranquil region and provides basic yet comfortable rooms with all the required conveniences. Guests may hire bicycles to explore the island, visit the well-known Anse Source d'Argent beach, or enjoy a leisurely walk through the verdant countryside. The welcoming hosts provide a warm welcome and are always willing to share advice and suggestions for making the most of your visit.

Unique Accommodations: Overwater Bungalows and Treehouses in Seychelles.

Seychelles, a gem in the Indian Ocean, is known for its beautiful beaches, lush scenery, and one-of-a-kind facilities that provide an exceptional vacation experience. Among them, overwater bungalows and treehouses stand out for their unique combination of luxury and nature.

While Seychelles is known for its coastal bungalows, actual overwater bungalows are uncommon. However, the adjacent islands and resorts have some of the most spectacular beachfront and oceanfront homes that give you the sensation of being above the sea. One such location is the Six Senses Zil Pasyon on Félicité Island. This resort has exquisite villas located on the island's edge, each with its infinity pool that seems to blend with the ocean. The villas are meant to fit in with the natural surroundings, creating a feeling of calm and privacy. The resort also provides a variety of activities, including snorkeling and diving, as well as yoga and wellness treatments, to provide a complete experience.

For those looking for a one-of-a-kind vacation among the trees, the Four Seasons Resort Seychelles on Mahé Island has magnificent treehouse villas. Nestled on the verdant hillside, these homes provide stunning views of the blue seas and the surrounding forest. Each villa has a private plunge pool, extensive living rooms, and high-end facilities. The resort's spa, perched high on the hill, provides treatments that combine local ingredients and ancient methods, resulting in a wonderfully revitalizing experience. Dining at the Four Seasons is a gourmet voyage, with restaurants serving Creole, Asian, and international cuisine.

Another excellent alternative is the North Island, a private island resort with both beachfront and hillside homes. The beachfront villas are only steps from the beautiful beaches, while the hillside villas are set amid the trees and have panoramic views of the ocean. Each house is constructed with sustainability in mind, including local materials and traditional workmanship. The resort is dedicated to conservation, with initiatives designed to maintain the island's unique flora and animals. Guests may engage in a variety of activities, including guided nature excursions, scuba diving, and kayaking.

The Raffles Seychelles on Praslin Island provides magnificent villas with private plunge pools and beautiful Indian Ocean views. The resort is located on a hillside and has villas that are intended for optimum seclusion and comfort. The Raffles Spa, situated on the hilltop, provides a variety of treatments inspired by the island's natural beauty. Dining at Raffles is a treat, with restaurants presenting a wide range of cuisines from fresh seafood to foreign specialties. The resort also provides a variety of sports, such as snorkeling, diving, and island trips.

For a more personal vacation, the JA Enchanted Island Resort provides individual villas on a tiny island in the Ste. Anne Marine National Park. These villas are fashioned in a typical Creole style and have private pools and direct beach access. The resort's restaurant provides Creole and international cuisine with fresh local ingredients. Guests may explore the marine park, snorkel or kayak, or just rest on the beach and enjoy the natural splendor.

Tips for Choosing the Best Accommodation in the Seychelles

Given the abundance of alternatives available throughout the Seychelles' 115 islands, selecting the ideal hotel can be both enjoyable and difficult. Whether you choose luxury, mid-range comfort, or low-cost accommodation, here are some pointers to help you discover the perfect location to lay your head in this tropical paradise.

First, assess the location. Mahé, Praslin, and La Digue are the three major islands in the Seychelles, each with its own distinct experience. The biggest island, Mahé, is home to the capital, Victoria, and has a variety of vibrant marketplaces, cultural attractions, and beautiful beaches. If you prefer a more peaceful environment, Praslin is famed for its gorgeous beaches, including Anse Lazio and the UNESCO-listed Vallée de Mai Nature Reserve. La Digue, with its laid-back feel and the famed Anse Source d'Argent beach, is ideal for visitors seeking to escape the rush and bustle.

Next, consider what sort of lodging best matches your travel style. Luxury resorts, such as the Four

Seasons Resort Seychelles and Six Senses Zil Pasyon, provide unprecedented extravagance with private villas, infinity pools, and world-class cuisine. For a more intimate experience, boutique hotels and guesthouses like Blue Hill and Takamaka Green Village provide individual service and a welcoming environment. Budget tourists will find comfort at establishments such as Bel Air Hotel and Captain's Villa, which provide basic facilities without sacrificing quality.

Amenities are another important consideration. If you're planning a romantic holiday, seek lodgings with private pools, spa services, and gourmet restaurants. Families may choose resorts with children's clubs, many food choices, and convenient access to beaches. Adventurers like lodgings that provide or are near to activities such as snorkeling, diving, and trekking. Always check to see whether the hotel has free Wi-Fi, breakfast, and other amenities that might help you enjoy your stay.

Reviews from other tourists might give useful information. Websites like TripAdvisor, Booking.com, and Expedia are excellent resources for learning about other visitors' experiences. Pay attention to feedback on cleanliness, service, and the general vibe of the establishment. Reviews might also reveal possible flaws that may not be visible on the hotel's website.

Seasonality may influence both supply and pricing. Seychelles has a tropical climate year-round, however, the busiest tourist seasons are December to January and June to August. Booking in advance during these times can result in lower rates and availability. If your vacation dates are flexible, try going during the shoulder seasons (April-May and October-November), when the weather is still great but the islands are less busy and lodging is frequently less expensive.

Finally, sustainability is becoming more essential to many tourists. Look for eco-friendly lodgings that use renewable energy, help local communities, and promote conservation. Resorts such as North Island and Six Senses Zil Pasyon are noted for their dedication to sustainability, providing exquisite accommodations while simultaneously benefiting the environment.

Shopping and Souvenirs

Local markets and craft shops in the Seychelles

Nestled in the center of the Indian Ocean, the Seychelles archipelago is not only a sanctuary of beautiful beaches and turquoise oceans but also a thriving cluster of local markets and artisan stores that provide a unique peek into the island's rich history and past. As you meander around these lively marketplaces, you'll get immersed in the everyday lives of the Seychellois, surrounded by the sights, sounds, and fragrances that distinguish this tropical paradise.

Begin your adventure at Victoria, the main city of Mahé Island, where the Sir Selwyn Selwyn-Clarke Market exemplifies the island's vibrant personality. This market, sometimes referred to as Victoria Market, is a sensory treat. It is open every day except Sunday and provides an excellent opportunity to learn about the local culture. Vendors proudly showcase their fresh food, which ranges from vivid tropical fruits to a variety of spices that fill the air with scent. The market also sells handcrafted items such as complex jewelry, bright fabrics, and wonderfully carved wooden souvenirs. Each piece offers a tale about the island's many cultural influences and artisanal traditions.

For those wanting a more private shopping experience, the handmade stores spread over the islands provide a delightful option. On Mahé, visit the Camion Hall Craft Centre, where local artists demonstrate their skills. This charming shop sells one-of-a-kind presents like hand-painted silk scarves and traditional Creole ceramics. The artists here are typically ready to explain the tales behind their pieces, which adds a personal touch to the purchasing experience.

Praslin Island, famed for its beautiful beaches and the famous Vallée de Mai Nature Reserve, also has several charming handmade businesses. The Black Pearl Farm and Boutique is a must-see, featuring magnificent jewelry crafted from locally sourced black pearls. Each item is a work of art that expresses the spirit of the water that surrounds these islands. Another hidden treasure on Praslin is Rita's Art Studio and Gallery, which has bright paintings and sculptures depicting the island's natural beauty and cultural legacy.

La Digue, the third biggest island, is not to be overlooked. Its relaxed ambiance and scenic settings make it an ideal setting for visiting local markets and artisan businesses. The island's main market, situated near the dock, is a smaller but just as lovely counterpart of Victoria Market. Fresh vegetables, spices, and a variety of handcrafted items are available here. The island also has various boutique stores where local artisans offer their products, such as handwoven baskets and beautiful shell jewelry.

While visiting these marketplaces and businesses, it is essential to observe sensible travel habits. Support local craftsmen by buying their handcrafted items, which not only give unique keepsakes but also contribute to the local economy. Consider the environmental effect of your purchases, choosing eco-friendly alternatives and avoiding things derived from endangered animals.

Top souvenirs to bring home from Seychelles

When you visit the wonderful Seychelles, you can't resist the temptation to carry a piece of this paradise home with you. The islands have an abundance of one-of-a-kind souvenirs that encapsulate the spirit of their colorful culture and breathtaking natural beauty. As you visit the local markets and boutique stores, you'll come across a range of keepsakes that make excellent souvenifor of your Seychellois journey.

One of the most memorable mementos to bring home is the Coco de Mer. This uncommon and unusual double coconut, found on the islands of Praslin and Curieuse, is an emblem of the Seychelles. Its distinctive form and size make it an intriguing discussion piece. To guarantee that you are supporting sustainable practices, acquire it from approved suppliers and receive the relevant export authorization.

Seychelles is well-known for its magnificent jewelry, which appeals to individuals with a refined taste. The Black Pearl Farm on Praslin sells beautiful jewelry made from locally produced black pearls. Each item is a tribute to the ocean's splendor, making it an ideal present or personal treasure. Additionally, Kreolor Jewelry, a premium brand, exhibits traditional workmanship by fusing natural elements from the Indian Ocean with 18-karat gold.

Art enthusiasts will find a home in the Seychelles, where indigenous artists are inspired by the islands' lush surroundings and colorful culture. Visit the galleries of renowned painters such as George Camille and Michael Adams to discover paintings and sculptures that reflect the essence of the Seychelles. These artworks are more than simply mementos; they are bits of the island's character, ready to be displayed in your house.

Handmade items are another appealing choice. Natural materials such as wood, coconut husks, and shells may be found in abundance in markets and craft stores. From finely carved wooden sculptures to hand-painted linens, these crafts showcase the island's rich artisanal past. The Camion Hall Craft Centre in Victoria is an excellent spot to begin your quest for these one-of-a-kind things.

No vacation to the Seychelles would be complete without trying and bringing back some of the local specialties. Takamaka Rum, made in Mahé, is a popular option. This locally made rum comes in a variety of tastes, with each bottle capturing a taste of the islands. Combine it with some Seychellois tea, which is noted for its fragrant mixes, to make the ideal gift combination.

Consider buying Seychellois vanilla to add a touch of class. This high-quality vanilla is cultivated on the islands and is known for its rich taste. It's an excellent complement to any kitchen and a fragrant remembrance of your stay in the Seychelles.

Finally, do not overlook the colorful batik textiles. These hand-dyed fabrics, with their vivid and vibrant motifs, are ideal for apparel, accessories, and home décor. They are a lovely way to bring a little of the island's creative flare with you.

Shopping Tips: What to Look For in Seychelles

Shopping the Seychelles is an experience in and of itself, with a delicious combination of local markets, boutique boutiques, and one-of-a-kind items that reflect the islands' vibrant culture and natural beauty. Whether you're wandering through Victoria's busy streets or discovering the calmer nooks of Praslin and La Digue, here are some pointers to help you make the most of your shopping trip.

First and foremost, it is critical to understand what to search for. The Seychelles are famed for its Coco de Mer, a unique and unusual double coconut found on the islands of Praslin and Curieuse. This one-of-a-kind keepsake is a must-have, but only from approved merchants and with the requisite export authorization to promote sustainable practices.

Another gem to search for is locally made jewelry. The Black Pearl Farm on Praslin produces magnificent jewelry from black pearls cultivated in the surrounding seas. These pearls are not only gorgeous but also represent the island's relationship to the water. Additionally, Kreolor Jewelry demonstrates traditional workmanship utilizing natural elements from the Indian Ocean mixed with 18-karat gold, resulting in a magnificent remembrance.

Art aficionados will find lots to appreciate in the Seychelles. Local artists are inspired by the islands' lush environment and lively culture to create amazing paintings and sculptures. Galleries like George Camille's and Michael Adams' are ideal for purchasing Seychellois art. These artworks are more than simply mementos; they are bits of the island's character, ready to be displayed in your house.

Handmade items are another attraction of Seychelles shopping. Natural materials such as wood, coconut husks, and shells may be found in abundance in markets and craft stores. From finely carved wooden sculptures to hand-painted linens, these crafts showcase the island's rich artisanal past. The Camion Hall Craft Centre in Victoria is an excellent spot to begin your quest for these one-of-a-kind things.

Takamaka Rum is a must-try for anyone seeking local tastes. Produced on Mahé, this locally distilled rum comes in a variety of tastes, with each bottle delivering a taste of the island. Combine it with some Seychellois tea, which is noted for its fragrant mixes, to make the ideal gift combination. Consider buying Seychellois vanilla to add a touch of class. This high-quality vanilla is cultivated on the islands and treasured for its rich taste, making it an ideal complement to any cuisine.

Batik clothes are another lovely keepsake to seek for. These hand-dyed fabrics, with their vivid and vibrant motifs, are ideal for apparel, accessories, and home décor. They are a lovely way to bring a little of the island's creative flare with you.

When shopping, remember to support local craftsmen and businesses. Each purchase supports the local economy and protects the Seychelles' unique legacy. Consider the environmental effect of your purchases, choosing eco-friendly alternatives and avoiding things derived from endangered animals.

Duty-Free Shops and Boutiques in Seychelles

When you arrive in the Seychelles, the attraction of duty-free shopping and boutique browsing is difficult to resist. The islands provide a lovely combination of luxury products, native crafts, and unusual treasures that make ideal souvenirs or presents. Whether you're at the airport or strolling the gorgeous streets of Victoria, here's all you need to know about shopping in this tropical paradise.

Seychelles International Airport, situated on Mahé Island, serves as your entry to duty-free shopping. SDuty-Freeree stores may be found throughout the arrival and departure halls. These establishments are ideal for tourists wishing to buy last-minute presents or indulge a in little retail therapy before their trip. The collection is excellent, ranging from luxury brands to locally crafted treasures. Perfumes, cosmetics, alcohol, and chocolates are all available at duty-free costs. It's the ideal spot to purchase a bottle of Takamaka Rum, a local favorite, or some Seychellois vanilla to take home.

For those who appreciate luxury, JOUEL at Kenwyn House in Victoria is a must-see. This store sells a wonderful collection of fine jewelry, timepieces, and decorations that reflect the brilliant colors and lovely shapes of the Seychelles. Each item is meticulously created, making it the ideal souvenir from your vacation. The beautiful designs often combine natural features from the islands, resulting in a distinctive combination of luxury and local charm.

Victoria, the capital city, also hseveral of boutique boutiques that appeal to a wide range of preferences and budgets. The Sir Selwyn Selwyn-Clarke Market, which is most renowned for its fresh vegetables and spices, also has booths offering homemade crafts and gifts. Everything here, from beautifully carved wooden sculptures to colorful fabrics, reflects the island's rich cultural legacy.

On Praslin Island, the Black Pearl Farm and Boutique is a must-see for jewelry connoisseurs. This business sells magnificent jewelry made of locally sourced black pearls, each one a monument to the ocean's splendor. The jewelry on display here is not only stunning, but it also serves as a memorable remembrance of your visit to the Seychelles.

La Digue, with its laid-back atmosphere, provides a more relaxing shopping experience. The primary market on the island, located near the jetty, is a smaller but no less lovely counterpart of Victoria Market. Fresh vegetables, spices, and a variety of handcrafted items are available here. The island also has various boutique stores where local artisans offer their products, such as handwoven baskets and beautiful shell jewelry.

As you visit these shopping places, remember to support local craftsmen and businesses. Each purchase supports the local economy and protects the Seychelles' unique legacy. Consider the environmental effect of your purchases, choosing eco-friendly alternatives and avoiding things derived from endangered animals.

Sustainable and Ethical Purchases in Seychelles

The Seychelles archipelago, located in the center of the Indian Ocean, is not just a beach lover's dream, but also a shining example of sustainable and ethical tourism. As you visit these beautiful islands, you will come across several possibilities to make purchases that benefit local people and the environment. Here's a guide for shopping wisely and ethically in the Seychelles.

Begin your tour in Victoria, the lively capital of Mahé Island. The Sir Selwyn Selwyn-Clarke Market is a dynamic center where you can discover a wide range of sustainable items. Look for vendors offering handcrafted items created from natural materials such as coconut husks, wood, and shells. These things are not only gorgeous but also ecologically beneficial since they are made using sustainable processes. The market is also an excellent location to get organic spices and locally produced food, which helps local farmers and lowers your carbon footprint.

The Camion Hall Craft Centre in Victoria offers a more refined shopping experience. This lovely location is home to various craftspeople who produce one-of-a-kind things utilizing traditional techniques. From hand-painted silk scarves to elaborate jewelry, each piece offers a narrative about the island's diverse cultural past. By buying these handcrafted items, you directly support the local economy and assisin in preservingve traditional crafts.

Those interested in sustainable jewelry can visit the Black Pearl Farm and Boutique on Praslin Island. The farm provides stunning black pearls that are grown utilizing ecologically safe practices. Each piece of jewelry is a tribute to the ocean's beauty and a reminder of the significance of safeguarding marine life. The store also sells a variety of other sustainable things, such as organic skincare produced using local ingredients.

La Digue, noted for its laid-back attitude and beautiful beaches, provides a more relaxing shopping experience. The primary market on the island, located near the jetty, is a smaller but no less lovely counterpart of Victoria Market. Fresh food, spices, and homemade crafts are all available here. Look for things made of recycled materials, such as bags and accessories fashioned from discarded fishing nets. These items not only decrease trash but also provide revenue for local artists.

Consider buying souvenirs certified by the Sustainable Seychelles Brand. This accreditation assures that the items satisfy the highest environmental and social responsibility criteria. Look for the emblem on products including apparel, accessories, and home décor. By purchasing certified items, you are supporting companies that value sustainability and ethical standards.

Takamaka Rum Distillery on Mahé is another excellent sustainable purchasing choice. This locally owned distillery makes a variety of rums using traditional processes and locally obtained ingredients. The distillery is dedicated to environmental techniques, such as employing renewable energy and minimizing trash. A bottle of Takamaka Rum is an ideal present or a delightful memento of your stay in the Seychelles.

As you travel the islands, keep an eye out for environmentally friendly items and companies that promote sustainability. Making mindful choices may help preserve the environment while also supporting the local economy. Remember to avoid anything created from endangered animals or unsustainable materials, and always inquire about the source of any products you purchase.

Day Tours & Excursions

Exploring the Inner Islands of Seychelles

Exploring the Inner Islands of Seychelles is like walking into a live postcard, with each turn revealing a fresh bit of beauty. Nestled in the center of the Indian Ocean, these islands entice people from all over with their lush scenery, gorgeous beaches, and lively local culture.

Start your tour in Mahé, the archipelago's biggest island and entrance. Mahé is home to the capital city, Victoria, where you can meander through lively marketplaces, see the renowned clock tower, and explore the lovely botanical gardens. The island's hilly interior, with its lush woods and hiking routes, offers a stark contrast to the seaside splendor. Don't pass up the opportunity to relax on Beau Vallon Beach, a popular hangout for both residents and tourists.

A short boat trip from Mahé will take you to Praslin, the second-largest island. Praslin is known for the

Vallée de Mai, a UNESCO World Heritage site that resembles an ancient woodland. The unique coco de mer palm may be found here, along with its large, suggestively formed nuts. The island's beaches, such as Anse Lazio and Anse Georgette, are often rated as among the world's greatest, with fluffy white sand and crystal-clear seas ideal for swimming and snorkeling.

Next, visit La Digue, where time seems to slow down. This island is well-known for its relaxed atmosphere and beautiful beaches, such as Anse Source d'Argent, which has spectacular granite rocks and shallow, blue seas. Rent a bicycle and discover the island's lovely towns and secret bays. La Digue's modest size makes it simple to get about, and the friendly residents are always ready with a grin and a tale.

Curieuse Island, located only a short boat ride from Praslin, offers a taste of adventure. This island is a home for gigantic tortoises, who wander freely in a safe environment. Curieuse also has lovely beaches and mangrove woods, making it ideal for trekking and animal watching. The island's past as a former leper colony lends an extra degree of mystery to your stay.

Aride Island is a must-visit for nature lovers. This island is a birdwatcher's heaven, with a diverse range of seabirds, including the uncommon roseate tern. The island's conservation efforts guarantee that its natural beauty is preserved, offering a haven for both birds and tourists seeking peace.

For those seeking luxury, Félicité Island has exquisite resorts that fit nicely with the natural surroundings. Enjoy world-class facilities while taking in the stunning vistas and private beaches. It's the ideal spot to relax and enjoy the calm beauty of the Seychelles.

Throughout your tour, you will be greeted with great hospitality by the Seychellois, whose Creole culture is a dynamic blend of African, European, and Asian elements. Savor the native cuisine, which includes fresh seafood, tropical fruits, and fragrant spices. Try grilled fish, octopus curry, and the famed breadfruit chips.

When exploring the Inner Islands, it's important to travel responsibly. Respect the local environment by reducing your effect, supporting conservation activities, and staying in eco-friendly lodgings. The Seychelles' dedication to sustainability guarantees that future generations may enjoy the country's natural beauty.

Marine Park Tours & Boat Cruises in the Seychelles.

Going on a marine park trip or boat ride in Seychelles is like entering a beautiful underwater world filled with life and color. The archipelago's marine parks are a biodiversity hotspot, providing a rare look into the underwater treasures.

Start your tour by visiting the Sainte Anne Marine National Park, which is just a short boat ride from Mahé. This park, founded in 1973, is one of the oldest marine reserves in the Indian Ocean. It includes six islands: Sainte Anne, Cerf, Round, Moyenne, Long, and Île Cachée. The crystal-clear waters here are ideal for snorkeling and diving, showing a rainbow of coral reefs, colorful fish, and the odd sea turtle. A guided catamaran cruise is a popular way to visit the park, with stops at numerous islands for swimming, snorkeling, and beachfront barbecues.

For a more personal encounter, visit Curieuse Island, which is noted for its enormous tortoises and history. Curieuse, once a leper colony, is now a protected sanctuary where these gentle giants may walk freely. A boat excursion to Curieuse often includes a visit to the tortoise sanctuary, a guided stroll through the mangrove woods, and several chances to snorkel in the nearby seas. The island's crimson soil and distinctive vegetation contribute to its unearthly allure.

Cousin Island is another must-see site for wildlife enthusiasts. This protected reserve provides a sanctuary for seabirds and a breeding ground for hawksbill turtles. Boat visits to Cousin are often guided by skilled experts who provide information about the island's conservation initiatives and rich species. The island's beautiful beaches and crystal blue seas make it an excellent location for snorkeling and birding.

For those looking for a luxury retreat, Félicité Island provides special boat tours that cater to your every want. These excursions often include visits to surrounding islands like Coco and Sister, where you may swim in hidden coves and eat gourmet meals made on-board. The crystal-clear waters near Félicité are home to an incredible variety of marine life, making it a snorkeler's dream.

No vacation to Seychelles is complete without seeing the Aldabra Atoll, a UNESCO World Heritage site and one of the world's biggest coral atolls. While more isolated and less popular with visitors, a boat journey to Aldabra is a once-in-a-lifetime adventure. The atoll's lagoons are rich with marine life, including manta rays, sharks, and other fish species. The atoll also has the world's biggest population of giant tortoises, making it a very unique site.

Throughout your aquatic experiences, you will be welcomed to great hospitality by the Seychellois. Local guides are proud of their islands and ready to share their expertise in the aquatic environment. Whether you're snorkeling among colorful fish, finding secret coves, or just resting on a beautiful beach, the splendor of Seychelles' marine parks will leave you speechless.

When exploring these underwater beauties, it's essential to travel properly. Respect the delicate marine ecosystems by avoiding harming the coral or upsetting the creatures. Choose environmentally friendly excursions that emphasize sustainability and conservation. You will be helping to guarantee that future generations may enjoy Seychelles' natural beauty.

Cultural and Historical Tours of Seychelles

Exploring Seychelles' cultural and historical tapestry is like peeling back the layers of a complex novel. This archipelago, famed for its beautiful beaches and verdant surroundings, also has a rich history and culture that begs to be explored.

Begin your tour at Victoria, the main city of Mahé Island. Victoria is one of the world's smallest capitals, yet it is full of charm and character. Begin at the Victoria Market, a thriving marketplace where people sell fresh food, spices, and fish. The market is a sensory experience, with brilliant colors and fragrances of tropical fruits and Creole spices filling the air. Nearby, the Clock Tower, a duplicate of London's Vauxhall Clock Tower, serves as a reminder of Seychelles' colonial history.

A short stroll from the market leads to the Seychelles National Museum of History. Here, you may learn about the archipelago's history, from its early settlers to the colonial period and beyond. The displays contain artifacts, images, and papers that provide a vivid picture of the islands' development. The museum also showcases Creole culture, which combines African, European, and Asian elements in local music, dance, and food.

The Mission Lodge offers a more in-depth look at the island's colonial past. Perched high in the Mahé highlands, this spot provides stunning views of the island's west coast. The lodge was formerly a school for the children of liberated slaves; now, its remains serve as a heartbreaking reminder of Seychelles' tangled past. The tranquil settings and panoramic views make it an ideal location for introspection.

On Praslin Island, the Vallée de Mai is a must-see. This UNESCO World Heritage Site is frequently referred to as a living museum. The old forest is home to the unique coco de mer palm, whose massive seeds are an emblem of Seychelles. Walking through the Vallée de Mai is like stepping back in time, with towering palm trees and dense vegetation creating an almost prehistoric environment. The place is also popular among birdwatchers, with species such as the black parrot adding to the charm.

La Digue Island provides a look into the traditional Seychellois lifestyle. Visit the L'Union Estate, a former coconut and vanilla plantation that has been designated as a Cultural Heritage Site. There's a classic copra mill, a colonial-era plantation home, and enormous tortoises wandering freely. The estate also contains the gorgeous Anse Source d'Argent beach, which is famed for its magnificent granite rocks and crystal blue seas.

Plan your trip around one of the Seychelles' numerous festivals for a unique cultural experience. The Creole Festival, celebrated annually in October, is a lively celebration of Creole culture. The event includes music, dancing, cuisine, and art, all of which highlight the Seychellois people's rich cultural history. Another highlight is the Seychelles Carnival, a colorful celebration that draws together entertainers from all over the globe for a boisterous march through Victoria's streets.

Throughout your cultural and historical tour, you will be met with great hospitality from the Seychellois people. Their tales, customs, and way of life are essential to the island's allure. Whether you're meandering through a lively market, visiting a historical monument, or taking part in a local festival, you'll have a better understanding of the rich cultural tapestry that distinguishes Seychelles.

Wildlife and Ecotourism Day Trips in Seychelles

Wildlife and eco-tourism day tours in the Seychelles are like entering a natural paradise, with surprising discoveries around every turn. The archipelago's dedication to conservation and sustainability makes it an ideal location for environmentally concerned tourists looking to connect with nature.

Begin your trip on Mahé, the biggest island, where Morne Seychellois National Park awaits. This enormous park encompasses more than 20% of the island and has a network of paths that go through lush woods, past flowing waterfalls, and panoramic vistas. The trek to Morne Blanc is especially rewarding, offering stunning views of the island and the surrounding seas. Along the trip, look for endemic species such as the Seychelles blue pigeon and Seychelles bulbul.

From Mahé, take a short boat journey to Sainte Anne Marine National Park, a marine sanctuary. Snorkeling and diving here show a thriving underwater environment teaming with beautiful coral reefs, tropical fish, and the odd sea turtle. The park's clean seas and various marine habitats make it a must-see for anybody involved in marine conservation. Guided trips often include stops at other islands inside the park, where you may explore beautiful beaches and have a picnic.

The Vallée de Mai, located on Praslin Island, is a UNESCO World Heritage site that transports visitors back in time. This old woodland is home to the unique coco de mer palm, whose massive seeds are an emblem of Seychelles. Walking through the Vallée de Mai, you'll be surrounded by towering palm trees and the sounds of indigenous species such as the black parrot. The forest's distinct ecology and significance in conservation make it an appealing destination for eco-tourists.

Curieuse Island, home to a colony of giant tortoises, offers a closer nature encounter. These gentle giants walk freely on the island, and a visit to the tortoise sanctuary provides an opportunity to learn about conservation efforts to safeguard these amazing species. Curieuse also has lovely beaches and mangrove woods, making it ideal for trekking and animal watching. The island's past as a former leper colony lends an interesting dimension to your stay.

Cousin Island is another treasure for nature lovers. This unique reserve protects seabirds and serves as a breeding location for hawksbill turtles. Cousin Island guided tours are given by expert conservationists who offer information about the island's environment and current animal protection activities. The island's beautiful beaches and crystal blue seas make it an excellent location for snorkeling and birding

For those looking for a more distant experience, the Aldabra Atoll, a UNESCO World Heritage site, is one of the world's biggest coral atolls. While more difficult to access, a day journey to Aldabra is a once-in-a-lifetime opportunity. The atoll's lagoons are rich with marine life, including manta rays, sharks, and other fish species. The atoll also has the world's biggest population of giant tortoises, making it a very unique site.

Throughout your eco-tourism experience, you will be welcomed to great hospitality by the Seychellois. Local guides are devoted to their islands and ready to share their expertise in the natural surroundings. Whether you're trekking through lush woods, diving amid beautiful coral reefs, or seeing animals in their native home, the splendor of Seychelles' ecosystems will astound you.

Travel carefully as you discover these natural treasures. Respect delicate ecosystems by avoiding disturbing animals or harming coral reefs. Choose environmentally friendly excursions that emphasize sustainability and conservation. You will be helping to guarantee that future generations may enjoy Seychelles' natural beauty.

Relaxing Spa & Wellness Retreats in the Seychelles

Indulging in a spa and wellness resort in Seychelles is like entering a calm sanctuary, where the pressures of daily life fade away among the islands' breathtaking natural beauty. The archipelago's luxury resorts and quiet environs provide the ideal environment for regeneration and relaxation.

Start your health adventure at the Constance Ephelia on Mahé Island. Nestled between two of the island's most gorgeous beaches, this resort has a full spa village to meet all of your relaxation requirements. The spa offers a range of services, ranging from conventional massages to innovative therapies, all aimed at relaxing your body and mind. The verdant surroundings and the sound of the ocean provide a relaxing ambiance ideal for unwinding. After your treatment, enjoy a leisurely walk around the resort's tropical gardens or unwind by the pool with a refreshing beverage.

For a more personal encounter, visit Anantara Maia Seychelles Villas. This resort, located on an isolated peninsula in Mahé, provides unrivaled solitude and luxury. Each villa has its own infinity pool and specialized butler service to ensure that all of your needs are satisfied. The resort's spa provides a variety of treatments inspired by local traditions and natural ingredients. Whether you select a relaxing massage or a refreshing facial, you will feel fully revitalized. The resort's breathtaking views of the Indian Ocean and calm environment make it an excellent spot to unwind and rejuvenate.

The Kempinski Seychelles Resort is located on Mahe's southwest shore. This seaside hideaway is nestled in a quiet harbor, providing a tranquil escape from the rush and bustle of everyday life. The resort's spa offers a range of services, including aromatherapy, hot stone massages, and purifying body wraps. The quiet surroundings and soft sound of the waves provide the ideal atmosphere for relaxation. After your spa treatment, take a relaxing dip in the resort's infinity pool or a stroll along the gorgeous beach.

For those looking for a complete wellness experience, the Avani Seychelles Barbarons Resort and Spa is an excellent option. This resort, located on Mahé's west coast, provides a variety of wellness programs aimed at promoting physical and emotional health. The spa offers a range of therapies, including yoga and meditation sessions, conventional massages, and cosmetic treatments. The resort's serene surroundings and emphasis on holistic health make it an excellent place for individuals seeking to revitalize both their bodies and minds.

Throughout your time in Seychelles, you will be greeted with great hospitality from the Seychellois people. The islanders' warm nature and passion for giving great service guarantee that your wellness vacation is an unforgettable experience. Whether you're having a peaceful massage, doing yoga on the beach, or just taking in the natural beauty of the islands, Seychelles provides the ideal setting for relaxation and renewal.

Insider Tips and Hidden Gems.

Secret Beaches Off the Beaten Path in Seychelles

Nestled in the center of the Indian Ocean, the Seychelles archipelago is a treasure trove of secluded beaches that provide a peaceful respite from the well-traveled pathways. While the famed Anse Source d'Argent and Beau Vallon attract tourists, the genuine spirit of Seychelles is found on its lesser-known beaches, where solitude and pristine beauty rule supreme.

Anse Georgette, located on Praslin Island, is one such beauty. This remote cove, which can only be reached by boat or a picturesque 30-minute stroll through dense forest, rewards the adventurous visitor with pure white sands and crystal-clear seas. The travel itself is part of the thrill, meandering through lush landscapes brimming with life. Upon arrival, the beach opens like a secret paradise, frequently absent of the regular crowds, making it an ideal destination for people seeking peace and natural beauty.

On La Digue, Anse Marron has a more rustic appeal. This beach is difficult to access, requiring a guided journey across rugged terrain and deep vegetation. But the effort is worthwhile. Anse Marron is a breathtaking combination of polished granite rocks, small natural ponds, and a clean beach. The only noises here are the calm lapping of waves and the occasional cry of seagulls, giving off a strong sensation of seclusion.

For anyone visiting Mahé, Anse Major is a must-see. This beach is accessible by a scenic coastal stroll that begins at Bel Ombre. The walk meanders along the shore, providing stunning views of the ocean and the neighboring rocks. Anse Major is a tranquil haven, with turquoise waters ideal for snorkeling and a backdrop of lush hills providing plenty of shade for a relaxing afternoon.

Petite Anse, located on Mahé, is another hidden gem. This beach, located behind the opulent Four Seasons Resort, is available to the public and accessible by a steep but reasonable route. The beach is a crescent of soft sand surrounded by clear, calm waters suitable for swimming. The surrounding granite boulders and green hills contribute to its hidden attractiveness, making it a popular spot among those in the know.

When exploring the outlying islands, Anse La Passe on Silhouette Island provides a one-of-a-kind experience. This beach is part of a marine national park, which ensures its pristine status. The seas here are rich with marine life, making it an ideal snorkeling destination. The island is a nature lover's paradise, with lush woods and high hills giving a dramatic background to the tranquil beach.

Local hangouts: Where the locals go in Seychelles

When you venture beyond Seychelles' postcard-perfect beaches, you'll discover a thriving local culture with its distinct hangouts. These local favorites look into Seychelloi's daily life and a genuine experience that is distant from the standard tourist circuit.

Begin your tour in Victoria, the lively capital of Mahé Island. The Sir Selwyn Selwyn-Clarke Market is a hub of activity, especially on Saturday mornings. Locals visit this colorful market to purchase fresh fish, tropical fruits, and spices. The air is filled with vendor chatter and the aroma of Creole food. It's the ideal place to try local delicacies like grilled fish and coconut curry, as well as to buy spices to take home.

For a more relaxed atmosphere, go to Beau Vallon Beach in the late afternoon. This renowned site is enjoyed by both visitors and locals. As the sun sets, family and friends come for beach picnics, where laughter mixes with the soft lapping of waves. The beach comes alive with spontaneous football and volleyball games, while food vendors sell everything from fresh fruit to sizzling skewers of meat.

On the nights, the Katiolo Nightclub near the airport on Mahé is the place to be. This open-air club is popular among locals because of its vibrant atmosphere and diverse music. The tunes range from reggae to local sega, keeping everyone dancing till the early hours. It's an excellent place to meet with locals and enjoy the island's bustling nightlife.

On Praslin Island, the Café des Arts in Cote d'Or is a popular local hangout. This seaside café and restaurant is well-known for its relaxing atmosphere and breathtaking views. Locals gather here to relax with a cool Seybrew beer or drink and to eat fresh fish. The café often presents live music, which contributes to the laid-back, island atmosphere.

La Plaine St. André on Mahé offers a taste of local culture. The historic plantation house has been converted into a distillery and restaurant. It's a popular place for locals to meet for a relaxing lunch or dinner. The menu includes traditional Creole dishes made with fresh, local ingredients, and the distillery produces Takamaka Rum, a popular local beverage. Tours of the distillery provide insights into the island's rum-making traditions.

On La Digue, the Fish Trap Restaurant & Bar is a local favorite. This location, directly on the beach, is ideal for a leisurely supper with your toes on the sand. The menu includes a mix of Creole and international dishes, and the bar offers refreshing cocktails. It's an excellent location for watching the sunset and enjoying the laid-back island vibe.

Best Photography Spots in Seychelles

The Seychelles, with its breathtaking landscapes and vibrant culture, is a photographer's paradise. From pristine beaches to lush forests, every corner of this archipelago presents a unique photo opportunity. Let's look at some of the best spots to capture the essence of Seychelles.

Begin your photography tour on La Digue Island, the site of the renowned Anse Source d'Argent. This beach is known for its stunning granite rocks, pure white sand, and crystal-clear seas. The interplay of light and shadow on the rocks produces a dramatic view, particularly at dawn and sunset. The shallow seas make it ideal for underwater photography, catching the vivid marine life.

Next, go to Praslin Island and see Anse Lazio. Anse Lazio, regarded as one of the world's most beautiful beaches, has a breathtaking background of blue waves, rich foliage, and polished granite boulders. The beach is quite remote, which allows for plenty of undisturbed shooting. Early morning or late afternoon light highlights the natural beauty, making your images very outstanding.

The Vallée de Mai Nature Reserve is a must-see on Praslin. This UNESCO Universe Heritage site is a magnificent, primeval woodland that seems like entering another universe. The towering coco de mer palms, peculiar to the Seychelles, provide a canopy that filters sunlight, giving a lovely glow on the forest floor. The reserve also has uncommon birds, such as the Seychelles black parrot, which will add a touch of wildness to your portfolio.

Mission Lodge Lookout, located on Mahé Island, the biggest in the archipelago, has breathtaking panoramic views. Perched high in the highlands, this ancient monument offers panoramic views of the island's west coast. The remains of the ancient missionary school lend a historical element to your photographs, while the surrounding tropical jungle and distant ocean form a magnificent landscape.

Sauzier Waterfall on Mahé offers a fresh viewpoint. This waterfall, nestled in a tranquil woodland, drops into a natural pool surrounded by lush flora. The forest's mellow, diffused lighting makes it a perfect location for photographing nature's serene beauty.

The short climb to the waterfall also provides several possibilities for photographing the island's unique flora and animals.

Another must-see attraction on Mahé is Anse Intendance. This wild and untamed beach is noted for its tremendous surf and breathtaking landscape. The rugged coastline, with its towering palm trees and crashing surf, is a stark contrast to the more tranquil beaches. It's an excellent spot for capturing the Seychelles' raw, natural beauty.

For those interested in marine life, the Saint-Anne Marine National Park provides a wealth of underwater photographic possibilities. The park, which includes several small islands, is home to vibrant coral reefs and a wide variety of marine species. Snorkeling or diving here allows you to capture the vibrant underwater world, including schools of tropical fish and graceful sea turtles.

Finally, don't forget to visit the lesser-known Anse Marron on La Digue. This secluded beach, accessible only by guided hike, features a distinct combination of smooth granite boulders, shallow natural pools, and pristine sands. The feeling of remoteness and natural beauty make it an ideal location for capturing the spirit of the Seychelles.

Time Your Activities for the Best Experience in Seychelles

Timing your activities in Seychelles might be the difference between a decent vacation and an outstanding one. This tropical paradise, with its year-round warm weather, provides a variety of experiences that are best enjoyed at specific times of year. Here's a guide to help you plan your activities so you have the best possible experience.

Beach bliss and water sports

April and May, as well as October and November, are perfect months to relax on beautiful beaches or dive into crystal-clear seas. During these months, the weather is warm and humid, with little rain, making it ideal for beach activities and island exploration. The seas are calm, creating ideal conditions for snorkeling and diving. Visibility underwater is excellent, enabling you to fully enjoy the rich marine life and coral reefs.

Hikes & Nature Walks

If you enjoy hiking and exploring lush landscapes, the cooler, drier months of May through September are ideal. The temperatures are slightly lower (ranging from 24°C to 30°C), and the humidity is more manageable. Trails such as the Morne Blanc on Mahé provide breathtaking views and are less strenuous in these cooler temperatures. The Vallée de Mai on Praslin, with its ancient palm forest, is also a must-see during this period.

Fishing enthusiasts

Fishing in the Seychelles is available year-round, but the best catches are usually found between October and April. These months are ideal for deep-sea fishing, as species such as marlin, sailfish, and tuna are more plentiful. Charter a boat and head out into the deep blue for an exciting fishing trip.

Bird Watching

Birdwatchers will find April to October especially rewarding. This time corresponds to the breeding season for many of the islands' indigenous birds. Cousin Island, a unique reserve, provides a sanctuary for birds including the Seychelles warbler and magpie robin. The island's conservation initiatives guarantee that bird populations flourish, providing several possibilities for sightings.

Turtle Nesting

Witnessing turtle nesting is a magnificent experience, and the ideal months to do it are October through February. Hawksbill and green turtles have been found to nest at beaches such as Anse Intendance on Mahé and Anse Georgette on Praslin. Early morning or late evening treks along these beaches may reward you with sightings of turtles laying eggs or hatchlings making their way to the sea.

Cultural Festivals

To immerse yourself in the local culture, arrange your vacation around one of Seychelles' colorful festivals. The Carnaval International de Victoria in April is a boisterous event featuring music, dancing, and colorful parades. October's Festival Kreol celebrates Creole culture through food, music, and traditional crafts. These events offer a unique glimpse into the island's cultural fabric and are a feast for the senses.

Whale Shark Spotting

For those who are captivated by marine giants, the optimum time to see whale sharks is between October and December. These gentle giants travel through the seas around Seychelles, and various tour companies provide snorkeling and diving excursions to observe them up close. It's a once-in-a-lifetime opportunity to swim with these gorgeous animals.

Seychelles offers unique cultural experiences that only insiders know about.

Exploring the Seychelles offers more than just beautiful beaches and lush landscapes; it also allows you to immerse yourself in the rich cultural tapestry that distinguishes these islands. While many visitors stick to the well-known attractions, those who are knowledgeable look for experiences that reveal the true heart of Seychellois culture. Here are some insider tips for unique cultural experiences that will make your trip memorable.

Begin your journey in Victoria, the capital city of Mahé Island. While the city itself is charming, the true cultural treasures can be found in its hidden corners. One such location is the Victoria Market, also known as Sir Selwyn Selwyn-Clarke Market. This lively market is the city's lifeblood, where inhabitants shop for fresh food, fish, and spices. Wander among the vivid kiosks, talk to the friendly merchants, and try some local delights like breadfruit chips and coconut nougat. The market is extremely bustling on Saturday mornings, providing a real glimpse into Seychelloi's everyday life.

The Seychelles Natural Past Museum offers a more in-depth look at the island's past. This small but fascinating museum in Victoria celebrates the island's natural and cultural heritage. Exhibits include the Seychelles' distinctive flora and wildlife, as well as early immigrants' antiquities. It's a quiet spot that is frequently overlooked by tourists, offering a peaceful retreat to learn about the islands' history.

On Praslin Island, the Vallée de Mai Nature Reserve is both a natural wonder and a cultural treasure. This UNESCO World Heritage site is home to the renowned coco de mer palm, which produces the world's biggest seed. The reserve's mysterious forest, with its towering palms and rare species, has spawned local stories and folklore. Take a guided tour to hear these tales and learn more about the cultural importance of this unique environment.

For a fully immersive experience, go to La Digue Island and see L'Union Estate. This ancient property provides insight into the island's colonial history. Explore the antique copra mill and vanilla plantation, and see traditional boatbuilding processes in action. The estate also has the famed

Anse Source d'Argent beach, but the cultural events are what distinguish it. Don't miss the opportunity to observe the enormous tortoises that wander the grounds, which represent the Seychelles' natural heritage.

Food is an important element of Seychellois culture, and there's no better way to enjoy it than to dine at a local restaurant. Marie Antoinette's Restaurant is a well-known establishment in Mahé. This restaurant, located in a colonial-era structure, provides traditional Creole cuisine such as octopus curry, grilled fish, and bat stew. The recipes have been handed down through generations and provide a genuine flavor of Seychellois cuisine. The friendly, inviting environment makes it popular with both residents and tourists.

Attending a mouthy dance performance provides another one-of-a-kind cultural experience. This ancient dance, originating in African slave culture, is distinguished by rhythmic drumming and heartfelt singing. Performances are frequently held at local festivals and cultural events. The dance is a powerful expression of Seychellois identity and resilience, and watching it is an emotionally charged experience that connects you to the island's history and spirit.

For those interested in the spiritual side of Seychelles, a visit to the Arul Mihu Navasakthi Vinayagar Temple in Victoria is a must. This colorful Hindu temple, dedicated to Lord Ganesha, stands out with its vibrant architecture and intricate carvings. It's a place of worship for the local Hindu community and a testament to the island's cultural diversity. Visitors are encouraged to visit the temple and learn about the Hindu traditions performed here.

Finally, don't miss the opportunity to join in a local festival. The Festival Kreol, held annually in October, is the biggest cultural event in Seychelles. It celebrates Creole culture via song, dancing, gastronomy, and art. The festival is a vivid exhibition of the islands' history, with activities taking place throughout Mahé, Praslin, and La Digue. Joining the festivities is a fantastic way to experience the joyous spirit and rich traditions of the Seychellois people.

Conclusion

As your trip through our Seychelles travel guide draws to a conclusion, let your mind linger on the sun-drenched coasts and bright landscapes of this island paradise. The Seychelles is more than a location; it is a state of mind—a place where time stops, nature sings its most exquisite songs, and the basic pleasures of life are rediscovered.

From the granite rocks of Anse Source d'Argent to the wild beauty of Aldabra Atoll, the Seychelles provide a diverse range of experiences that extend well beyond its postcard-perfect beaches. It is a place where traditions are upheld, cultures merge, and sustainability is more than a goal—it is a way of life.

Whether you've basked in the turquoise seas, tasted Creole cuisine, or discovered the abundant marine life that lives under the waves, you've experienced the essence of the Seychelles: authenticity, peace, and amazement.

As you leave these islands, take with you not only memories of crystal-clear seas and swaying palms, but also a renewed sense of connection—to nature, others, and yourself. Allow the Seychelles to inspire you to seek beauty in the ordinary, to tread lightly on the Earth, and to embrace the joy of discovery wherever your travels take you.

Scan Qrcode to See Map

Printed in Great Britain
by Amazon

56935829R00126